Bond

Verbal Reasoning

Assessment Papers

11+–12+ years
Book 2

Jane Bayliss

Nelson Thornes

Published in 2011 by:
Nelson Thornes Ltd
Delta Place
27 Bath Road
CHELTENHAM
GL53 7TH
United Kingdom

13 / 10 9 8 7 6 5 4 3

A catalogue record for this book is available from the British Library

ISBN 978 1 4085 1606 5

Page make-up by Tech Set Ltd

Printed in China by 1010 Printing International Ltd.

Before you get started

What is Bond?

This book is part of the Bond Assessment Papers series for verbal reasoning, which provides a **thorough and progressive course in verbal reasoning** from ages six to twelve. It builds up verbal reasoning skills from book to book over the course of the series.

Bond's verbal reasoning resources are ideal preparation for the 11+ and other secondary school selection exams.

How does the scope of this book match real exam content?

Verbal Reasoning 11+-12+ Book 1 and *Book 2* are the advanced Bond 11+ books. Each paper is **pitched at a level above a typical 11+ exam**, providing greater challenges and stretching skills further. The papers practise a wide range of questions drawn from the four distinct groups of verbal reasoning question types: sorting words, selecting words, anagrams, coded sequences and logic. The papers are fully in line with 11+ and other selective exams for this age group but are designed to practise **a wider variety of skills and question types** than most other practice papers so that children are always challenged to think – and don't get bored repeating the same question type again and again. We believe that variety is the key to effective learning. It helps children 'think on their feet' and cope with the unexpected: it is surprising how often children come out of verbal reasoning exams having met question types they have not seen before.

What does the book contain?

- **10 papers** – each one contains 100 questions.
- **Tutorial links throughout** - 📖 – this icon appears in the margin next to the questions. It indicates links to the relevant section in *How to do ... 11+ Verbal Reasoning*, our invaluable subject guide that offers explanations and practice for all core question types.
- **Scoring devices** – there are score boxes in the margins and a Progress Chart on page 64. The chart is a visual and motivating way for children to see how they are doing. It also turns the score into a percentage that can help decide what to do next.
- **Next Steps Planner** – advice on what to do after finishing the papers can be found on the inside back cover.
- **Answers** – located in an easily-removed central pull-out section.

How can you use this book?

One of the great strengths of Bond Assessment Papers is their flexibility. They can be used at home, in school and by tutors to:

- set **timed formal practice** tests – allow about 45 minutes per paper in line with standard 11+ demands. Reduce the suggested time limit by five minutes to practise working at speed
- provide **bite-sized chunks** for regular practice
- **highlight strengths and weaknesses** in the core skills
- identify **individual needs**
- set **homework**
- follow **a complete 11+ preparation strategy** alongside *The Parents' Guide to the 11+* (see below).

It is best to start at the beginning and work through the papers in order. If you are using the book as part of a careful run-in to the 11+, we suggest that you also have two other essential Bond resources close at hand:

How to do ... 11+ Verbal Reasoning: the subject guide that explains all the question types practised in this book. Use the cross-reference icons to find the relevant sections.

The Parents' Guide to the 11+: the step-by-step guide to the whole 11+ experience. It clearly explains the 11+ process, provides guidance on how to assess children, helps you to set complete action plans for practice and explains how you can use the *Verbal Reasoning 11⁺-12⁺ Book 1* and *Book 2* as part of a strategic run-in to the exam.

See the inside front cover for more details of these books.

What does a score mean and how can it be improved?

It is unfortunately impossible to guarantee that a child will pass the 11+ exam if they achieve a certain score on any practice book or paper. Success on the day depends on a host of factors, including the scores of the other children sitting the test. However, we can give some guidance on what a score indicates and how to improve it.

If children colour in the Progress Chart on page 64, this will give an idea of present performance in percentage terms. The Next Steps Planner inside the back cover will help you to decide what to do next to help a child progress. It is always valuable to go over wrong answers with children. If they are having trouble with any particular question type, follow the tutorial links to *How to do ... 11+ Verbal Reasoning* for step-by-step explanations and further practice.

Don't forget the website...!

Visit www.bond11plus.co.uk for lots of advice, information and suggestions on everything to do with Bond, the 11+ and helping children to do their best, and exams.

Paper 1

Look at these groups of words.

A	B	C	D
travel	insects	time	liquids

Choose the correct group for each of the words below. Write in the letter.

1–5 luggage ___   vinegar ___   annual ___   midge ___

paraffin ___   modern ___   passenger ___   lemonade ___

flea ___   century ___

Underline two words, one from each group, that go together to form a new word. The word in the first group always comes first.

Example   (hand, <u>green</u>, for)   (light, <u>house</u>, sure)

6 (circle, ring, square)   (line, friend, leader)

7 (water, ride, trip)   (tap, fall, over)

8 (ice, snow, fog)   (drop, drip, mist)

9 (bright, dull, light)   (air, room, house)

10 (sea, son, sun)   (rose, rise, risk)

Find the letter which will end the first word and start the second word.

Example   peac (<u>h</u>) ome

11 par (___) ake

12 tal (___) ind

13 far (___) etre

14 kit (___) dge

15 sal (___) ooth

Find a word that is similar in meaning to the word in capital letters and that rhymes with the second word.

Example   CABLE   tyre   <u>wire</u>

16 CORRECT   light   _____

17 EARTH   sound   _____

18 TIMEPIECE   mock   _____

19 HINDER   scamper   _____

20 SHOAL   tool   _____

Underline the pair of words most similar in meaning.

B 5

Example   come, go   <u>roam, wander</u>   fear, fare

21 horde, mob   blunt, sharp   couple, single

22 gather, scatter   launch, begin   veto, allow

23 squander, save   firm, loose   entice, tempt

24 join, separate   grace, charm   novel, unoriginal

25 cease, begin   engrave, carve   mild, wild

5

Underline one word in the brackets which is most opposite in meaning to the word in capitals.

B 6

Example   WIDE   (broad vague long <u>narrow</u> motorway)

26 LEVEL   (straight flat smooth uneven horizontal)

27 FILLED   (empty full plenty stuffed whole)

28 PLACID   (silent motionless active calm stationary)

29 WAX   (enlarge rise wane swell develop)

30 ALLY   (partner friend mate colleague foe)

5

Rearrange the muddled letters in capitals to make a proper word. The answer will complete the sentence sensibly.

B 16

Example   A BEZAR is an animal with stripes.   <u>ZEBRA</u>

31 The two children AKWELD down the lane.   _____

32 The programme was too CYASR for young children.   _____

33 Luckily, she wasn't EJNRIUD in the accident.   _____

34 Olives grow on RETES.   _____

35 UDEIG means to escort someone.   _____

5

Find the three-letter word which can be added to the letters in capitals to make a new word. The new word will complete the sentence sensibly.

B 22

Example   The cat sprang onto the MO.   <u>USE</u>

36 The PFUL puppy followed the children around the garden.   _____

37 They invited the NEIGHBS round for a drink.   _____

38 He used CCHES for three weeks after breaking his toe.   _____

39 The FISMEN headed back to port to avoid the storm.   _____

40 The girl cried because her hamster had ESED.   _____

5

Move one letter from the first word and add it to the second word to make two new words.

B 13

Example   hunt   sip   <u>hut</u>   <u>snip</u>

41 sting   sea   _____   _____

42 paint   met   _____   _____

43 globe   race   _____   _____

44 pretty   each   _____   _____

45 clover   lava   _____   _____

5

Change the first word of the third pair in the same way as the other pairs to give a new word.

B 18

Example   bind, hind   bare, hare   but, <u>hut</u>

46 ever, eve   peace, pea   barren, _____

47 near, are   phase, sea   scar, _____

48 hat, hit   sat, sit   pat, _____

49 sent, nets   rite, tier   hems, _____

50 jet, jest   bet, best   wet, _____

5

Complete the following sentences by selecting the most sensible word from each group of words given in the brackets. Underline the words selected.

B 14

Example   The (<u>children</u>, books, foxes) carried the (houses, <u>books</u>, steps) home from the (greengrocer, <u>library</u>, factory).

51 The (kind, greedy, clever) (boy, dog, girl) wouldn't share his (sweets, socks, sister).

52 The cat (licked, scratched, kicked) the (oil, coffee, milk) from the (kettle, saucer, bed).

53 You can (draw, write, research) your (homework, sports, letter) on the (park, internet, envelope).

54 Mum (drove, swam, rush) to the (food, kitchen, garden) centre to buy new (plants, cars, books).

55 Please don't (watch, listen, play) (puzzles, football, drawing) near the (flowers, clouds, music).

5

A group of boys took an exam. Michael and Fahad received different marks, but their marks were both formed from the numbers 3 and 4. Michael had the lowest mark. Chen had 2 more than Michael, but 3 less than Abbas. Nicholas had eight more marks than Michael but 5 fewer than Misha.

B 25

Write the marks each boy got.

56 Michael   ___   57 Fahad   ___   58 Misha   ___

59 Chen   ___   60 Abbas   ___   61 Nicholas   ___

6

Fill in the crosswords so that all the given words are included. You have been given one letter as a clue in each crossword.

62–63

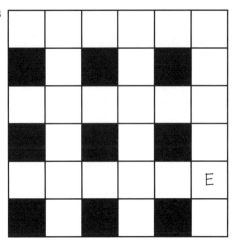

aspect, taster, endure, accrue,
talent, spades

64–65

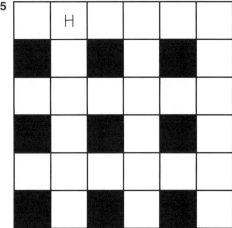

yields, hooray, offend, theory,
warned, toffee

If $a = 2$, $b = 3$, $c = 4$, $d = 5$, $e = 6$, find the answer to these calculations.

66 $eb =$ _____

67 $\dfrac{bc}{a} =$ _____

68 $\dfrac{4c}{a} =$ _____

69 $2ad =$ _____

70 $5d - 2a =$ _____

71 $\dfrac{2bc}{c} =$ _____

If the code for ILLUSTRATE is qrrstuvwux, what are the codes for the following words?

72 TREAT _____   **73** SLATE _____   **74** LEAST _____

What do these codes stand for?

75 vstu _____   **76** rwuxv _____

Give the two missing pairs of letters in the following sequences. The alphabet has been written out to help you.

A B C D E F G H I J K L M N O P Q R S T U V W X Y Z

	Example	CQ	DQ	EP	FP	*GO*	*HO*
77	ZD	XE	VF	___	RH	___
78	ED	___	II	KL	MN	___
79	AB	ZD	BG	___	CP	___
80	PL	QK	___	SI	TH	___

(4)

If the code for PINEAPPLE is $+ - \times \% \pounds + + @ \%$, what are the codes for the following words?

81 LEAP _____   **82** PLAIN _____   **83** LINE _____

What do these codes stand for?

84 $+ \pounds @ \%$ _____   **85** $@ \pounds \times \%$ _____   **86** $\times \pounds - @$ _____

(6)

Fill in the missing letters. The alphabet has been written out to help you.

A B C D E F G H I J K L M N O P Q R S T U V W X Y Z

Example   AB is to CD as PQ is to *RS*

87 JT is to LV as SU is to _____

88 XPE is to ZNG as MVG is to _____

89 ELT is to IPX as JAR is to _____

90 JDI is to HGG as PFW is to _____

91 AXD is to ZCW as BVQ is to _____

(5)

Read the first two statements and then underline one of the four options below that must be true.

92 'Ameena flew to Italy on an aeroplane. Ameena likes to fly.'

    Ameena went on holiday to Italy.

    Flying is the quickest way to travel.

    Some aeroplanes take passengers to Italy.

    Some people are nervous of flying.

Read the first statement and then underline one of the five options below that must be true.

93 'Children going on the trip were told to take a waterproof coat with them.'

Bad weather was forecast.

It usually rains in the autumn.

The children had to spend most of the day walking around.

Children were advised to take a particular item of clothing.

Comfortable shoes should also be worn.

Read the first statement and then underline one of the five options below that must be true.

94 'Some cats and dogs need to be groomed.'

Owners should always groom their pets.

Certain animals need to be groomed.

A brush is softer than a comb.

Dog hair makes a mess in the house.

Brushes and combs for animals can be bought in pet shops.

Read the first two statements and then underline one of the five options below that must be true.

95 'The bus arrives at school at 8:45 a.m. It usually leaves school about 3:30 p.m.'

Lessons start at 9:00 a.m.

The bus belongs to the school.

Most pupils use the school bus.

The bus doesn't always leave at 3:30 p.m.

Children who miss the bus must get their parents to collect them.

4

Find a word that can be put in front of each of the following words to make new, compound words.

B 11

Example	CAST	FALL	WARD	POUR	DOWN
96 WORD	BOW	OVER	BONES		_____
97 SHOW	BOARD	KICK	TRACK		_____
98 SIDE	SHOOT	STAGE	HAND		_____
99 LAW	SIDE	RAGE	WARD		_____
100 WATER	STAND	FOOT	LINE		_____

5

Now go to the Progress Chart to record your score!   Total ◯ **100**

6

Paper 2

Underline the word in the brackets closest in meaning to the word in capitals.

Example   UNHAPPY   (unkind death laughter <u>sad</u> friendly)

1 STILL   (busy soft loud quiet alone)

2 LONG   (thin brief high angry desire)

3 CALM   (wild peaceful excited stormy rough)

4 DISAPPEAR   (arrive come surface vanish emerge)

5 BRIEF   (lengthy hide wordy rambling curt)

Underline the one word in the brackets which will go equally well with both the pairs of words outside the brackets.

Example   rush, attack   cost, fee   (price, hasten, strike, <u>charge</u>, money)

6 receive, take   agree to, allow   (gain, obtain, believe, accept, approve)

7 dwelling, home   lecture, talk to   (house, address, location, speech, settle)

8 depart, migrate   touch, affect   (advance, impress, move, proceed, motivate)

9 condemn, attack   plague, burden   (disaster, ordeal, spell, curse, swear)

10 bathe, swim   decline, descend   (drop, dip, drench, damp, deck)

Find the three-letter word which can be added to the letters in capitals to make a new word. The new word will complete the sentence sensibly.

Example   The cat sprang onto the MO.   <u>USE</u>

11 Please DESCE everything you saw.   _____

12 Do you know if the house is VAT?   _____

13 The PE of lions slept in the shade.   _____

14 Adopt a more POIVE attitude to your work. _____

15 She ran to her parents' room after hearing a STGE noise downstairs. _____

Find the letter which will end the first word and start the second word.

Example   peac (<u>h</u>) ome

16 bur   (—) olk

17 sag   (—) lso

18 pin   (—) ven

19 cas   (—) not

20 fel   (—) aint

Change the first word into the last word, by changing one letter at a time and making a new, different word in the middle.

B 13

Example   CASE   _CASH_   LASH

21 MOST   _____   DUST

22 COST   _____   COAX

23 SAME   _____   HOME

24 LAMB   _____   GAME

25 FOUR   _____   POUT

 5

Rearrange the muddled letters in capitals to make a proper word. The answer will complete the sentence sensibly.

B 16

Example   A BEZAR is an animal with stripes.   _ZEBRA_

26 A pet rabbit lives in a TUHHC.   _____

27 Low ground between two hills is called a LYALVE.   _____

28 An PTOOIN is a choice.   _____

29 RTIHBG is the opposite of dull.   _____

30 Pasta is popular in LTYAI.   _____

 5

Underline the two words, one from each group, that go together to form a new word. The word in the first group always comes first.

B 8

Example   (hand, <u>green</u>, for)   (light, <u>house</u>, sure)

31 (with, wit, wish)   (on, in, it)

32 (door, house, key)   (fence, wood, board)

33 (more, last, price)   (cost, less, fix)

34 (life, watch, time)   (notice, guard, pass)

35 (arm, blaze, fight)   (are, our, hour)

 5

Complete the following sentences by selecting the most sensible word from each group of words given in the brackets. Underline the words selected.

B 14

Example   The (<u>children</u>, books, foxes) carried the (houses, <u>books</u>, steps) home from the (greengrocer, <u>library</u>, factory).

36 The (girl, bird, fish) put her (food, babies, gloves) on because it was (sunny, cold, sad).

37 A (swan, fox, spider) is a (sporty, wild, slippery) (reptile, person, mammal).

38 (Funny, older, modern) (pupils, patients, drivers) should start to think about their next (parents, schools, children).

39 The (text, letter, email) was sent to their (advanced, new, ringing) (station, bedroom, house).

40 You can (take, put, steal) the money from my (folder, book, purse) for your (crime, bus fare, police).

B 17

Find and underline the two words which need to change places for each sentence to make sense.

    Example   She went to <u>letter</u> the <u>write</u>.

41 Please try do to your corrections.

42 Remove it with the oven from care.

43 Dog the came in from the garden when it started to rain.

44 Let's tidy up because she will in here be a few minutes.

45 Will new clubs some be starting next term.

B 18

Change the first word of the third pair in the same way as the other pairs to give a new word.

    Example   bind, hind   bare, hare   but, <u>hut</u>

46 tarnish, tar   warden, war   beetle, _____

47 mountain, tan   project, jet   entire, _____

48 hostage, tag   suspend, pen   deride, _____

49 skip, sip   sway, say   buoy, _____

50 affair, air   excel, eel   avert, _____

B 19

Fill in the crosswords so that all the given words are included. You have been given one letter as a clue in each crossword.

51–52

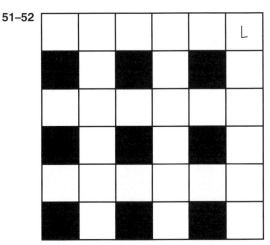

bridle, tonsil, owners, speedy, angers, losses

tokens, hungry, keener, reckon,
sketch, keeper

Fill in the missing letters. The alphabet has been written out to help you.

A B C D E F G H I J K L M N O P Q R S T U V W X Y Z

Example   AB is to CD as PQ is to RS

55 GOH is to IQJ as KSN is to _____

56 EJT is to GMX as BKP is to _____

57 CAH is to DZJ as MYP is to _____

58 BHV is to AGU as XKD is to _____

59 JZH is to LXJ as TCN is to _____

If the code for PECULIAR is 23456789, what are the codes for the following words?

60 RAIL   _____   61 PEAR   _____   62 PRICE   _____

What do these codes stand for?

63 4682   _____   64 9563   _____   65 2763   _____

Give the two missing pairs of letters in the following sequences. The alphabet has been written out to help you.

A B C D E F G H I J K L M N O P Q R S T U V W X Y Z

Example	CQ	DQ	EP	FP	GO	HO
66 KD	MG	OJ	___	___	US
67 PL	SI	VF	___	___	EW
68 NGQ	___	PES	QDT	RCU	___
69 ___	PUL	NSJ	LQH	___	HMD
70 ABC	EFG	___	MNO	QRS	___

I was three years old when my brother was born, and my sister was two years younger than me. Next year I will be twelve.

B 25

71 How old was I last year? _____

72 How old will my sister be next year? _____

73 How old will my brother be when my sister is twenty? _____

74 When my brother was six, how old was my sister? _____

4

Here are the number codes for five words. Match the right word to the right code.

B 24

4322	5123	4153	7653	5647
CURE	CELL	RULE	RICH	HIRE

75 CURE _____ **76** CELL _____ **77** RULE _____ **78** RICH _____ **79** HIRE _____

5

If $A = 1$, $B = 2$, $C = 3$, $D = 4$ and $E = 5$, give the answer to the following calculations.

B 26

80 $(D \div B) + E =$ _____

81 $2C =$ _____

82 $D^2 + B^2 =$ _____

83 $E + C - B =$ _____

84 $(B^2 + C^2) - (D^2 - C^2) =$ _____

85 $(C^2 \times B^2) + (E^2 - A^2) =$ _____

6

Find a word that is similar in meaning to the word in capital letters and that rhymes with the second word.

B 5

Example CABLE tyre *wire*

86 PURCHASE shy _____

87 SEAT stair _____

88 TALENT hair _____

89 POST frail _____

90 STICK flew _____

5

Complete the following expressions by underlining the missing word.

B 15

Example Frog is to tadpole as swan is to (duckling, baby, cygnet).

91 Sharp is to blunt as major is to (main, minor, superior).

92 Revise is to correct as cure is to (remedy, illness, disease).

93 Echo is to repeat as flaw is to (perfect, loud, fault).

94 Spare is to extra as sincere is to (false, deceitful, genuine).

95 Protect is to harm as abandon is to (desert, claim, keep).

5

Which word in each group contains only the first six letters of the alphabet? Underline the answer.

Example   defeat   farce   abide   <u>deaf</u>   dice

96 able   fade   cage   badge   each

97 dale   aback   deal   deed   beak

98 cake   bale   babe   cable   feel

99 behalf   acid   ache   cash   beef

100 dead   adage   action   cadge   frame

5

Now go to the Progress Chart to record your score!   Total   100

Paper 3

Look at these groups of words.

A	B	C	D
caterpillar	palace	herd	cousin
tadpole	house	pride	nephew
calf	bungalow	flock	sister

Choose the correct group for each of the words below. Write in the letter.

1–5 fawn ___   chalet ___   uncle ___   castle ___

igloo ___   swarm ___   parents ___   cub ___

gosling ___   litter ___

5

Find two letters which will end the first word and start the second word.

Example   rea (<u>c h</u>) air

6 plur (__ __) so

7 trav (__ __) egant

8 drea (__ __) stery

9 flow (__ __) ase

10 pala (__ __) nsor

5

Find the three-letter word which can be added to the letters in capitals to make a new word. The new word will complete the sentence sensibly.

Example   The cat sprang onto the MO.   USE

11 The weather was FLY good all day.   _____

12 My BHER cannot come out until he has tidied his room.   _____

13 Some children get BD during long school holidays.   _____

14 She wrote PRIE on the cover of her diary.   _____

15 I EFULLY noted down the telephone number.   _____   5

Underline the one word in the brackets which will go equally well with both the pairs of words outside the brackets.

Example   rush, attack   cost, fee   (price, hasten, strike, <u>charge</u>, money)

16 protect, shelter   lid, roof   (top, blanket, safe, cover, box)

17 unfriendly, hostile   foreign, different   (enemy, alien, abroad, separate, unusual)

18 finish, end   whole, undivided   (achieved, all, total, close, complete)

19 goodwill, kindness   approval, prefer   (like, favour, service, back, spoil)

20 outburst, row   place, site   (circumstances, location, outlook, scene, tantrum)   5

Underline the two words, one from each group, which are closest in meaning.

Example   (race, shop, <u>start</u>)   (finish, <u>begin</u>, end)

21 (control, convenience, effort)   (discomfort, confusion, ease)

22 (temper, bright, reassure)   (depress, encourage, endear)

23 (futile, affect, banish)   (profitable, admit, fruitless)

24 (mind, merge, club)   (mix, divide, social)

25 (commute, place, inhabit)   (household, occupy, resident)   5

Find the four-letter word hidden at the end of one word and the beginning of the next word. The order of the letters may not be changed.

Example   The children had bats and balls.   sand

26 Don't drop lotion on the towel.   _____

27 That match appeared live on television.   _____

28 We often hear children playing in the street.   _____

29 I made all the cakes for Connor's birthday party.   _____

30 I am aiming to finish this by Friday.   _____   5

Find and underline the two words which need to change places for each sentence to make sense.

Example   She went to <u>letter</u> the <u>write</u>.

31 I can't concentrate on the television is when.

32 In month the weather has been sunnier than this August.

33 I must water the plants while you am out.

34 She is saving a money to buy her new hamster cage.

35 Don't hear off until you set the whistle blow.

Underline the two words which are the odd ones out in the following groups of words.

Example	black	<u>king</u>	purple	green	<u>house</u>
36 duck	waddles	eagle	nest		heron
37 local	alien	foreigner	native		stranger
38 post	letter	column	newspaper		stake
39 idle	busy	lazy	foolish		unproductive
40 windy	snowing	pretty	horrible		raining

Read the first two statements and then underline one of the five options below that must be true.

41 'Elena's father is Italian. Her father's parents still live in Italy.'

        Elena can speak Italian.

        Elena goes to Italy at least once a year.

        Elena's father no longer lives in Italy.

        Elena has grandparents who live in Italy.

        Rome is the capital of Italy.

Read the first two statements and then underline one of the five options below that must be true.

42 'My sister is expecting a baby. The baby might be a girl.'

        My sister would rather have a girl.

        My sister has bought pink baby clothes.

        The doctor thinks it's a girl.

        Doctors work in hospitals.

        My sister might have a boy.

Read the first two statements and then underline one of the five options below that must be true.

43 'Many people have cars. Some buy expensive cars.'

People prefer cheaper cars.

Some people have expensive cars.

Old cars usually cost less.

Sports cars are always expensive.

Expensive cars use a lot of petrol.

Read the first two statements and then underline one of the five options below that must be true.

44 'Year 6 pupils went on a trip to France. Most mornings they went to the bakery.'

France is famous for nice bread.

The children bought bread at the bakery.

The children spoke French in the bakery.

Bread is eaten with jam for breakfast.

Sometimes the children went to the bakery.

Look at the first group of three words. The word in the middle has been made from the other two words. Complete the second group of three words in the same way, making a new word in the middle.

Example	PAIN	INTO	TOOK	ALSO	<u>SOON</u>	ONLY
45 LEFT	TALE	SACK	KEEL	———	FILM
46 LONG	GOAL	FAIL	CALF	———	ACNE
47 GRIP	PAGE	DEAF	SAID	———	STUN
48 BYTE	BEAT	CAKE	EACH	———	WISP
49 URGE	BEAR	BAIL	IDEA	———	CROP
50 BOARD	SOLD	CLOSE	LEASE	———	PRIDE

Complete the following sentences by selecting the most sensible word from each group of words given in the brackets. Underline the words selected.

Example The (<u>children</u>, books, foxes) carried the (houses, <u>books</u>, steps) home from the (greengrocer, <u>library</u>, factory).

51 I (hurt, looked, cheated) my (book, finger, window) playing (homework, texting, netball).

52 Please (make, buy, sell) some (ham, cake, sweets) and I'll make us a (mess, drink, sandwich) for lunch.

15

53 Our (grandmother, baby, tree) will be (years, thousands, seventy) next (minute, day, week).

54 Over the (last, present, next) few years I have (went, come, been) to the cinema (frequently, slowly, unusually).

55 If you (scribble, take, send) lots of (sketches, stories, texts), your parents will (reward, complain, smile) about the bill.

5

Fill in the crosswords so that all the given words are included. You have been given one letter as a clue in each crossword.

B 19

56–57

recede, deceit, annexe, client,
fennel, severe

58–59

temple, stress, staple, breeds,
rarest, barter

4

Give the missing numbers in the following sequences.

	Example	2	4	6	8	<u>10</u>	<u>12</u>
60	40	80	35	88		___	___
61	3	3	6	18		___	360
62	14	16	19	___	28		___
63	___	23	16	10	___		1
64	___	58	45	34	25		___

On the street below live five families. The Li family live in a house with an even number. The Wilmots are on the same side of the street as the Journeauxs but are not next door to them. The Singhs live across the street from the Hicks and next door to the Wilmots. The Journeauxs house looks onto the park.

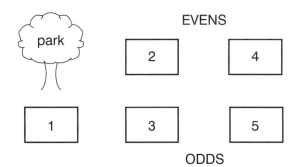

Write the name of the family that lives in each of the following houses.

65 1   ___   **66** 2   ___   **67** 3   ___

68 4   ___   **69** 5   ___

If the code for INCUBATE is @ £ $ + % − × 0, what are the codes for the following words?

70 BITE   ___   **71** ACT   ___   **72** CABIN   ___

What do these codes stand for?

73 × + % 0   ___   **74** % 0 − ×   ___   **75** × + £ 0   ___

Which one letter can be added to the front of all the words to make new words?

Example	care	cat	crate	call

76	__ell	__hap	__harm	__heat	__heck
77	__ilt	__ill	__ike	__oarse	__uddle
78	__ose	__uff	__rove	__roud	__ick
79	__haw	__est	__ale	__aper	__aut
80	__ell	__arn	__ard	__ield	__outh

5

If A = 2, B = 4, C = 5, D = 6, E = 8 and F = 9, find the sum of the following words by adding the letters together.

81 BEAD _____   82 FADE _____

83 FEED _____   84 CEDE _____

85 DEAF _____

5

Underline the two words, one from each group, which are the most opposite in meaning.

Example	(dawn, early, wake)	(late, stop, sunrise)

86 (exaggerate, exact, expand)   (definite, enlarge, imprecise)

87 (security, isolate, insult)   (offend, praise, upset)

88 (ever, extra, moor)   (more, always, never)

89 (rarity, common, ready)   (shortage, frequency, eager)

90 (flashing, shouting, hazardous)   (uncertain, safe, warning)

5

Remove one letter from the word in capital letters to leave a new word. The meaning of the new word is given in the clue.

Example	AUNT	an insect	ant

91 CLASH   money   _____

92 STORMY   legend   _____

93 BARGE   exposed   _____

94 WAIVE   use hand in greeting   _____

95 KNIT   equipment   _____

5

Underline the two words which are made from the same letters.

Example	TAP	PET	<u>TEA</u>	POT	<u>EAT</u>
96 PACK	CARE	CARP	RACK	RACE
97 FIST	SOFT	HOST	THAT	SHOT
98 STEEL	STALL	LEAST	STALE	TEASE
99 ONCE	NONE	CONES	NEON	SCORE
100 ANTLER	ANTHEM	TALENT	LEARNT	THEME

5

Now go to the Progress Chart to record your score! **Total** **100**

Paper 4

Underline one word in the brackets which is most opposite in meaning to the word in capitals.

Example WIDE (broad vague long <u>narrow</u> motorway)

1 FOOLISH (wise crazy absurd simple weak)

2 BOOK (album note register cancel reserve)

3 SOCIABLE (hostile outgoing approachable organised serious)

4 FIERCE (cruel aggressive gentle intense grim)

5 PERFECT (excellent flawed exact ideal entire)

5

Underline the one word in the brackets which will go equally well with both the pairs of words outside the brackets.

Example rush, attack cost, fee (price, hasten, strike, <u>charge</u>, money)

6 answer, explanation — liquid, mixture — (key, response, blend, solution, settle)

7 register, file — achievement, personal best — (account, record, report, track, performance)

8 issue, concern — important, count — (subject, event, matter, stuff, worry)

9 rub, scrape — bars, fireplace — (burn, fuel, grind, grate, scratch)

10 quick, brisk — cross, irritable — (hasty, lively, sluggish, snappy, snarling)

5

19

Find the three-letter word which can be added to the letters in capitals to make a new word. The new word will complete the sentence sensibly.

B 22

Example   The cat sprang onto the MO.   USE

11 She took her prescription straight to the CIST.   _____

12 INGIENTS are usually listed at the start of a recipe.   _____

13 We RLY watch our old videos.   _____

14 Luckily most local INHAANTS were moved to safety before the volcano erupted.   _____

15 Adequate PREPAION is essential before any exam.   _____

5

Find two letters which will end the first word and start the second word.

B 10

Example   rea (c h) air

16 cra (_ _) ade

17 sha (_ _) sh

18 spa (_ _) corate

19 tr (_ _) rie

20 ma (_ _) side

5

Underline the one word in the brackets closest in meaning to the word in capitals.

B 5

Example   UNHAPPY   (unkind death laughter sad friendly)

21 ANSWER   (responsible question argue respond tick)

22 COMMON   (grass garden weed unusual ordinary)

23 PROBLEM   (sum hard solution difficulty impossible)

24 FIND   (lose reward discover decision evidence)

25 PART   (divide fracture whole chorus play)

5

Find a word that can be put in front of each of the following words to make new, compound words.

B 11

Example   CAST   FALL   WARD   POUR   DOWN

26 COURT   CAST   GO   GROUND   _____

27 LIKE   BIRTH   HOOD   MINDER   _____

28 BOARD   BAND   LIGHT   STONE   _____

29 LANCE   WAY   WHEEL   STYLE   _____

30 LETTER   FLASH   PAPER   AGENT   _____

5

Complete the following sentences by selecting the most sensible word from each group of words given in the brackets. Underline the words selected.

B 14

Example The (<u>children</u>, books, foxes) carried the (houses, <u>books</u>, steps) home from the (greengrocer, <u>library</u>, factory).

31 The (child, children, pupil) argue about (which, what, who) can use the (timetable, outing, computer).

32 We can go (by, past, through) train to the (stick, match, burn) next (tomorrow, yesterday, week).

33 My dog is losing the (sound, taste, sight) in her (right, correct, wrong) (leg, tail, eye).

34 Can I go to (village, country, town) with my (pets, friends, enemies) after (school, dentist, shop)?

35 Don't (play, use, mention) the (email, calculator, radio) to do these (sums, pictures, art).

5

Complete the following expressions by underlining the missing word.

B 15

Example Frog is to tadpole as swan is to (duckling, baby, <u>cygnet</u>).

36 Sensible is to reasonable as childish is to (family, trusting, immature, perfect, weak).

37 Bad is to evil as good is to (fresh, wicked, skilled, worthy, corrupt).

38 Glare is to scowl as spot is to (clean, clothes, skin, eye, see).

39 Temporary is to permanent as eternal is to (changeable, heaven, airy, endless, undying).

40 Rapid is to fast as slow is to (hectic, rushed, quiet, hurried, leisurely).

5

Rearrange the muddled letters in capitals to make a proper word. The answer will complete the sentence sensibly.

B 16

Example A BEZAR is an animal with stripes. *ZEBRA*

41 A CHEAP is a type of summer fruit. _____

42 A MASTER is a small river. _____

43 TRAINS is to stretch or draw tight. _____

44 A VIRAL is someone against whom one competes. _____

45 STOAT is to brown something, such as a piece of bread. _____

5

Underline two words, one from each group, that go together to form a new word. The word in the first group always comes first.

B 8

Example (hand, <u>green</u>, for) (light, <u>house</u>, sure)

46 (all, never, ever) (body, less, green)

47 (tail, meet, slow) (wag, or, up)

48 (all, whole, half) (low, day, way)

49 (ship, pay, bread) (role, slip, meant)

50 (not, note, cub) (now, able, board)

5

knuckle   kinetic   kindle   kidney   kettle

51 Which word contains the letter nearest to the end of the alphabet? _____

52 Which word has the most vowels in it? _____

53 Which vowel is used in all the words? _____

54 Which letter occurs once in KIDNEY and KINDLE and twice in KINETIC? _____

55 Write the words in alphabetical order.

_____   _____   _____   _____   _____

Fill in the crosswords so that all the given words are included. You have been given one letter as a clue in each crossword.

56–57

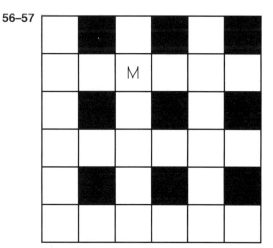

sleepy, dispel, number, people,
embers, unused

58–59

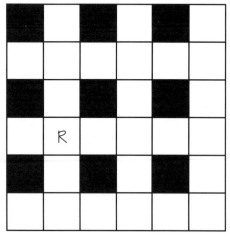

bikini, adhere, rewind, aspire,
braise, learns

Give the missing numbers in the following sequences.

B 23

Example   2   4   6   8   <u>10</u>   <u>12</u>

60 15   15   16   18   ___   ___

61 33   36   40   43   ___   ___

62 48   9   24   ___   ___   36

63 ___   64   ___   36   25   16

64 8   16   ___   24   24   ___

5

If the code for FRAGMENT is PSUWCXZG, what are the codes for the following words?

B 24

65 GEAR   _____   **66** FRAME _____   **67** GATE   _____

What do these codes stand for?

68 PXUS   _____   **69** GUCX _____   **70** SUPG   _____

6

If A = 4, B = 6, C = 5, D = 8 and E = 3, give the answers to these calculations as letters.

B 26

71 $A \times B = D \times$?   ___

72 $A^2 = E + C +$?   ___

73 $(D \times E) + B = ? \times C$ ___

74 $A + B + E = ? + D$ ___

75 $B^2 - A^2 = C \times$?   ___

5

Change the first word of the third pair in the same way as the other pairs to give a new word.

B 18

Example   bind, hind   bare, hare   but, <u>hut</u>

76 kink, ink   late, ate   pour, _____

77 lamb, lame   comb, come   hard, _____

78 debit, bite   medal, dale   petal, _____

79 frail, grail   crown, drown   soil, _____

80 alter, tear   ember, beer   expel, _____

5

Here are the number codes for six words. Match the right word to the right code.

B 24

1634	3527	2534	3641	2633	4653
FALL	FILM	LAMP	LIFT	MAIL	PALM

81 FALL   _____   **82** FILM   _____   **83** LAMP   _____

84 LIFT   _____   **85** MAIL   _____   **86** PALM   _____

6

Read the first two statements and then underline one of the five options below that must be true.

87 'Fractions are sums. Some children find fractions hard.'

Fractions are always hard.

Most children like maths.

Children should be able to do fractions.

Children find certain sums hard.

It's easier to use a calculator for difficult sums.

Read the first two statements and then underline one of the five options below that must be true.

88 'Jamille plans to catch the bus into town at 11:30 a.m. The bus can be up to 10 minutes late.'

Jamille knows he will have to wait for the bus.

Public transport is often reliable.

Jamille will be late to meet his friends.

The bus will have arrived by 11:40 a.m.

Jamille prefers his mum to take him in the car.

Read the first two statements and then underline one of the five options below that must be true.

89 'Sarah is 17 years old. You can learn to drive at 17.'

Sarah has started driving lessons.

Most people start learning to drive at 17.

It is best to have lessons from a qualified instructor.

Sarah's parents have bought her a car.

Sarah can now learn to drive.

Read the first two statements and then underline one of the five options below that must be true.

90 'Sprouts are green. Sprouts are vegetables.'

Carrots are not green.

Not all vegetables are green.

Sprouts are green vegetables.

Sprouts are sold in supermarkets.

Green vegetables are good for you.

4

A, B, C, D and E have mobile phones.

A and E have pink phones, the others have silver ones.

B, D and E can access the internet on their phones, the others cannot.

A, B and E just send text messages, the others text and make calls.

91 Who has a silver phone used just for texting?   _____

92 Who has internet access on a pink phone?   _____

93 Who has a silver phone, but no internet access?   _____

94 Who has internet access and makes calls?   _____

4

Fill in the missing letters. The alphabet has been written out to help you.

A B C D E F G H I J K L M N O P Q R S T U V W X Y Z

Example   AB is to CD as PQ is to RS

95 GI is to JF as NK is to   _____

96 BU is to CV as HM is to   _____

97 QJ is to SM as FO is to   _____

98 WX is to DC as ZY is to   _____

99 UG is to TF as ME is to   _____

100 BW is to AX as ZZ is to   _____

6

Now go to the Progress Chart to record your score!   Total   100

Paper 5

Underline the two words, one from each group, which are closest in meaning.

Example   (race, shop, start)   (finish, begin, end)

1 (defer, defend, define)   (shift, shield, attack)

2 (distress, remote, remove)   (comfort, alert, distant)

3 (hint, advice, gossip)   (helper, notify, trace)

4 (paper, administration, stationary)   (pens, computer, immobile)

5 (fine, lovely, nice)   (clever, thick, thin)

5

Underline the pair of words most opposite in meaning.

B 9

Example   cup, mug   coffee, milk   <u>hot, cold</u>

6   company, firm   compete, contend   dislike, prefer

7   ideal, best   splendid, drab   disarray, chaos

8   picture, imagine   intention, goal   interest, boredom

9   provide, remove   publish, print   health, diet

10 regal, noble   primitive, developed   priceless, costly

5

Find the three-letter word which can be added to the letters in capitals to make a new word. The new word will complete the sentence sensibly.

B 22

Example   The cat sprang onto the MO.   <u>USE</u>

11 What time does the train DEP?   _____

12 The foal trotted along beside its MOT.   _____

13 It takes a lot of COUE to sing on your own in a concert.   _____

14 I'm amazed that you managed to do the LE test.   _____

15 If you play football at lunchtime, your school TRORS will get dirty.   _____

5

Change the first word into the last word by changing one letter at a time and making a new, different word in the middle.

B 13

Example   CASE   <u>CASH</u>   LASH

16 WIND   _____   SINK

17 DOZE   _____   MAZE

18 SAIL   _____   SAND

19 DOTE   _____   LOVE

20 TOLD   _____   ROAD

5

Complete the following sentences by selecting the most sensible word from each group of words given in the brackets. Underline the words selected.

B 14

Example   The (<u>children</u>, books, foxes) carried the (houses, <u>books</u>, steps) home from the (greengrocer, <u>library</u>, factory).

21 She (watched, scored, marked) the correct (answer, idea, effort) with a (cross, dot, tick).

22 The puppy was (licked, fed, trained) to (bite, sit, scratch) (lively, quietly, noisily).

23 He (left, bought, gave) his (cat, sweater, soap) in the (library, fridge, oven).

24 (Grass, Smoke, Plastic) melts (in, out, off) extreme (cold, ice, heat).

25 We need to (fetch, get, look) you a new (glove, boot, coat) for the (spell, winter, weathered).

5

Find the four-letter word hidden at the end of one word and the beginning of the next word. The order of the letters may not be changed.

    Example   The children had bats and balls.   <u>sand</u>

26 He chose to have a swimming party.   ————

27 The head teacher is dealing with an issue affecting every class.   ————

28 He climbed over the fence and jumped down onto the grass.   ————

29 After school we sometimes ride about the park on our bikes.   ————

30 Staff offer individual pupils help if needed.   ————   **5**

Look at the first group of three words. The word in the middle has been made from the other two words. Complete the second group of three words in the same way, making a new word in the middle.

Example	PAIN	INTO	T<u>OO</u>K	ALSO	<u>SOON</u>	ONLY	
31 HIDE	MAID	NAME		ITEM	————	FIST	
32 SORRY	ROSE	SENSE		MOANS	————	NAÏVE	
33 TREK	LATE	NAIL		FATE	————	LAIR	
34 RAIL	RATE	TEAR		PAIN	————	AREA	
35 REAL	HARE	HEEL		WEAN	————	FOND	
36 PIPE	COPE	CODE		RULE	————	RAIN	**6**

Find the letter which will complete both pairs of words, ending the first word and starting the second. The same letter must be used for both pairs of words.

    Example   mea (<u>t</u>) able   fi (<u>t</u>) ub

37 dee (—) efy   woo (—) eck

38 plat (—) vent   crat (—) nvy

39 chil (—) ead   coi (—) atch

40 shar (—) ost   was (—) ump

41 boa (—) ole   moo (—) eal   **5**

Move one letter from the first word and add it to the second word to make two new words.

    Example   hunt   sip   <u>hut</u>   <u>snip</u>

42 caper   eel   ————   ————

43 niche   sift   ————   ————

44 tang   tee   ————   ————

45 raft   rail   ————   ————

46 sidle   pay   ————   ————   **5**

Complete the following expressions by underlining the missing word.

Example   Frog is to tadpole as swan is to (duckling, baby, <u>cygnet</u>).

47 Cow is to beef as pig is to (sty, piglet, pork, grunt, farm).

48 Sleep is to slept as go is to (come, going, travel, went, goodbye).

49 Boat is to water as car is to (garage, road, driver, petrol, fast).

50 Eager is to keen as essential is to (needless, indispensable, nonsense, useless, normal).

51 Pleasure is to pain as crooked is to (bent, curved, crafty, shady, straight).

Underline the word in the brackets which goes best with the words given outside the brackets.

Example   word, paragraph, sentence   (pen, cap, <u>letter</u>, top, stop)

52 oak, fir   (bluebell, primrose, palm, parsley, bean)

53 serious, grave   (absurd, helpless, solemn, lazy, foolish)

54 quarrel, disagree   (settle, satisfy, permit, allow, dispute)

55 midnight, dawn   (atmosphere, cloudy, horizon, sunset, planet)

56 greet, salute   (ignore, welcome, frighten, march, pleased)

Underline the two words which are the odd ones out in the following groups of words.

Example   black   <u>king</u>   purple   green   <u>house</u>

57 cheap   expensive   dear   loved   costly

58 breed   type   raise   lower   nurture

59 total   number   question   increase   add

60 wind   blow   thump   damage   punch

61 author   poem   sketch   poet   artist

Find and underline the two words which need to change places for each sentence to make sense.

Example   She went to <u>letter</u> the <u>write</u>.

62 Polish must you your shoes before tomorrow.

63 The sun came just out after lunch.

64 It is now too complicated to explain far.

65 Add the teabag and remove some milk.

66 She made one new friends after just two day.

Underline two words, one from each group, that go together to form a new word. The word in the first group always comes first.

Example   (hand, <u>green</u>, for)   (light, <u>house</u>, sure)

67 (rest, wonder, ward)   (full, ore, den)

68 (car, sand, on)   (our, pit, nest)

69 (split, miss, bar)   (gin, row, take)

70 (writ, bite, grow)   (err, up, ten)

71 (up, prop, red)   (shore, dish, pose)

B 8

5

Which one letter can be added to the front of all these words to make new words?

B 12

Example   <u>c</u>are   <u>c</u>at   <u>c</u>rate   <u>c</u>all

72 ___each   ___eact   ___ead   ___ear   ___eign

73 ___ack   ___alt   ___eed   ___uit   ___igh

74 ___rim   ___art   ___uff   ___ark   ___ick

75 ___eat   ___ush   ___aul   ___ack   ___and

76 ___ury   ___ulky   ___oom   ___est   ___ank

5

Fill in the crosswords so that all the given words are included. You have been given one letter as a clue in each crossword.

B 19

77–78

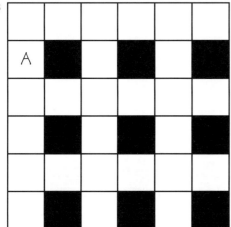

engine, ravage, morsel, rivals,
island, margin

29

pander, sweets, trains, marrow,
wrists, advise

Give the two missing pairs of letters in the following sequences. The alphabet has been written out to help you.

A B C D E F G H I J K L M N O P Q R S T U V W X Y Z

Example	CQ	DQ	EP	FP	<u>GO</u>	<u>HO</u>
81 PX	QW	____	SU	TT	____	
82 DH	EI	GK	JN	____	____	
83 AC	TB	BA	SZ	____	____	
84 ____	SG	QI	OK	MM	____	
85 EF	HI	KL	NO	____	____	

If the code for DOCUMENT is ! × + @ ? £ O =, what are the codes for the following words?

86 CODE _____   87 TEND _____

88 DUET _____   89 TUNE _____

What do these codes stand for?

90 O @ = _____   91 + × ? £ _____

92 ! @ O £ _____   93 O × = £ _____

If S = 2, W = 3, R = 4, B = 5 and N = 6, find the answers to the following calculations.

94 $(S \times W) + N =$ _____   95 $R + N - S =$ _____   96 $B^2 - R^2 =$ _____

97 $2S + W^2 =$ _____   98 $2N + 3W =$ _____   99 $N - S + W =$ _____

100 $(B \times S) + W =$ _____

4

B 23

5

B 24

8

B 26

7

Paper 1

1. luggage – A, vinegar – D
2. annual – C, midge – B
3. paraffin – D, modern – C
4. passenger – A, lemonade – D
5. flea – B, century – C
6. ringleader
7. waterfall
8. snowdrop
9. lighthouse
10. sunrise
11. t
12. k
13. m
14. e
15. t
16. right
17. ground
18. clock
19. hamper
20. school
21. horde, mob
22. launch, begin
23. entice, tempt
24. grace, charm
25. engrave, carve
26. uneven
27. empty
28. active
29. wane
30. foe
31. WALKED
32. SCARY
33. INJURED
34. TREES
35. GUIDE
36. LAY
37. OUR
38. RUT
39. HER
40. CAP
41. sing, seat
42. pint, meat
43. lobe, grace
44. petty, reach
45. clove, larva
46. bar
47. arc
48. pit
49. mesh
50. west
51. greedy, boy, sweets
52. licked, milk, saucer
53. research, homework, internet
54. drove, garden, plants
55. play, football, flowers
56. 34
57. 43
58. 47
59. 36
60. 39
61. 42

62–63

T	A	L	E	N	T
■	S	■	N	■	A
S	P	A	D	E	S
■	E	■	U	■	T
A	C	C	R	U	E
■	T	■	E	■	R

64–65

T	H	E	O	R	Y
■	O	■	F	■	I
T	O	F	F	E	E
■	R	■	E	■	L
W	A	R	N	E	D
■	Y	■	D	■	S

66. 18
67. 6
68. 8
69. 20
70. 21
71. 6
72. uvxwu
73. trwux
74. rxwtu
75. RUST
76. LATER
77. TG, PI
78. GG, OQ
79. YK, XV
80. RJ, UG
81. @%£+
82. +@£−×
83. @−×%
84. PALE
85. LANE
86. NAIL
87. UW
88. OTI
89. NEV
90. NIU
91. YEJ
92. Some aeroplanes take passengers to Italy.
93. Children were advised to take a particular item of clothing.
94. Certain animals need to be groomed.
95. The bus doesn't always leave at 3:30 p.m.
96. CROSS
97. SIDE
98. OFF
99. OUT
100. UNDER

Paper 2

1. quiet
2. desire
3. peaceful
4. vanish
5. curt
6. accept
7. address
8. move
9. curse
10. dip
11. RIB
12. CAN
13. RID
14. SIT
15. RAN
16. y
17. a
18. e
19. k
20. t
21. MUST
22. COAT
23. SOME
24. LAME
25. POUR
26. HUTCH
27. VALLEY
28. OPTION
29. BRIGHT
30. ITALY
31. within
32. keyboard
33. priceless
34. lifeguard
35. armour
36. girl, gloves, cold
37. fox, wild, mammal
38. older, pupils, schools
39. letter, new, house
40. take, purse, bus fare
41. do, to
42. with, from
43. Dog, the
44. in, be
45. will, some
46. bee
47. tie
48. rid
49. boy
50. art

51–52

T	O	N	S	I	L
■	W	■	P	■	O
A	N	G	E	R	S
■	E	■	E	■	S
B	R	I	D	L	E
■	S	■	Y	■	S

53–54

S	K	E	T	C	H
	E		O		U
R	E	C	K	O	N
	P		E		G
K	E	E	N	E	R
	R		S		Y

55 MUP
56 DNT
57 NXR
58 WJC
59 VAP
60 9876
61 2389
62 29743
63 CLAP
64 RULE
65 PILE
66 QM, SP
67 YC, BZ
68 OFR, SBV
69 RWN, JOF
70 IJK, UVW
71 10
72 10
73 19
74 7
75 4153
76 4322
77 5123
78 5647
79 7653
80 7
81 6
82 20
83 6
84 6
85 60
86 buy
87 chair
88 flair
89 mail
90 glue
91 minor
92 remedy
93 fault
94 genuine
95 keep
96 fade
97 deed
98 babe
99 beef
100 dead

Paper 3

1 fawn – A, chalet – B
2 uncle – D, castle – B
3 igloo – B, swarm – C
4 parents – D, cub – A

5 gosling – A, litter – C
6 al
7 el
8 my
9 er
10 ce
11 AIR
12 ROT
13 ORE
14 VAT
15 CAR
16 cover
17 alien
18 complete
19 favour
20 scene
21 convenience, ease
22 reassure, encourage
23 futile, fruitless
24 merge, mix
25 inhabit, occupy
26 plot
27 chap
28 arch
29 deal
30 maim
31 on, when
32 in, this
33 I, you
34 a, her
35 hear, set
36 waddles, nest
37 local, native
38 letter, newspaper
39 busy, foolish
40 pretty, horrible
41 Elena has grandparents who live in Italy.
42 My sister might have a boy.
43 Some people have expensive cars.
44 Sometimes the children went to the bakery.
45 LIKE
46 FACE
47 DUST
48 EPIC
49 CARD
50 DIRE
51 hurt, finger, netball
52 buy, ham, sandwich
53 grandmother, seventy, week
54 last, been, frequently
55 send, texts, complain

56–57

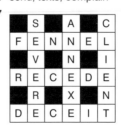

	S		A		C
F	E	N	N	E	L
	V		N		I
R	E	C	E	D	E
	R		X		N
D	E	C	E	I	T

58–59

	R		S		B
B	A	R	T	E	R
	R		A		E
T	E	M	P	L	E
	S		L		D
S	T	R	E	S	S

60 30, 96
61 72
62 23, 34
63 31, 5
64 73, 18
65 Journeaux
66 Hicks
67 Singh
68 Li
69 Wilmot
70 %@×0
71 −$×
72 $−%@£
73 TUBE
74 BEAT
75 TUNE
76 c
77 h
78 p
79 t
80 y
81 20
82 25
83 31
84 27
85 25
86 exact, imprecise
87 insult, praise
88 ever, never
89 rarity, frequency
90 hazardous, safe
91 cash
92 story
93 bare
94 wave
95 kit
96 CARE, RACE
97 HOST, SHOT
98 LEAST, STALE
99 NONE, NEON
100 ANTLER, LEARNT

Paper 4

1 wise
2 cancel
3 hostile
4 gentle
5 flawed
6 solution
7 record

ANSWERS

8 matter
9 grate
10 snappy
11 HEM
12 RED
13 ARE
14 BIT
15 RAT
16 sh
17 me
18 de
19 ee
20 in
21 respond
22 ordinary
23 difficulty
24 discover
25 divide
26 FORE
27 CHILD
28 HEAD
29 FREE
30 NEWS
31 children, who, computer
32 by, match, week
33 sight, right, eye
34 town, friends, school
35 use, calculator, sums
36 immature
37 worthy
38 see
39 changeable
40 leisurely
41 PEACH
42 STREAM
43 STRAIN
44 RIVAL
45 TOAST
46 evergreen
47 tailor
48 halfway
49 payslip
50 notable
51 kidney
52 kinetic
53 e
54 i
55 kettle, kidney, kindle, kinetic, knuckle

56–57

58–59

	L		B		A
R	E	W	I	N	D
	A		K		H
B	R	A	I	S	E
	N		N		R
A	S	P	I	R	E

60 21, 25
61 47, 50
62 18, 12
63 81, 49
64 16, 32
65 WXUS
66 PSUCX
67 WUGX
68 FEAR
69 TAME
70 RAFT
71 E
72 D
73 B
74 C
75 A
76 our
77 hare
78 tale
79 toil
80 peel
81 2633
82 2534
83 3641
84 3527
85 4653
86 1634
87 Children find certain sums hard.
88 The bus will have arrived by 11:40 a.m.
89 Sarah can now learn to drive.
90 Sprouts are green vegetables.
91 B
92 E
93 C
94 D
95 QH
96 IN
97 HR
98 AB or GD
99 LD
100 YA

Paper 5

1 defend, shield
2 remote, distant
3 hint, trace

4 stationary, immobile
5 fine, thin
6 dislike, prefer
7 splendid, drab
8 interest, boredom
9 provide, remove
10 primitive, developed
11 ART
12 HER
13 RAG
14 WHO
15 USE
16 WINK
17 DAZE
18 SAID
19 DOVE
20 TOAD
21 marked, answer, tick
22 trained, sit, quietly
23 left, sweater, library
24 plastic, in, heat
25 get, coat, winter
26 echo
27 than
28 dove
29 idea
30 rind
31 SITE
32 NONE
33 RAFT
34 PEAR
35 FAWN
36 RARE
37 d
38 e
39 l
40 p
41 r
42 cape, reel
43 nice, shift
44 tag, teen
45 rat, frail
46 side, play
47 pork
48 went
49 road
50 indispensable
51 straight
52 palm
53 solemn
54 dispute
55 sunset
56 welcome
57 cheap, loved
58 type, lower
59 question, number
60 wind, damage
61 poem, sketch

Bond Verbal Reasoning Assessment Papers 11+-12+ years Book 2

A3

62 polish, you
63 just, out
64 now, far
65 add, remove
66 one, two
67 restore
68 sandpit
69 barrow
70 written
71 reddish
72 r
73 s
74 p
75 h
76 b

77–78

M	O	R	S	E	L	
A		I		N		
R	A	V	A	G	E	
G		A		I		
I	S	L	A	N	D	
N		S		E		

79–80

	P		T		S
M	A	R	R	O	W
	N		A		E
A	D	V	I	S	E
	E		N		T
W	R	I	S	T	S

81 RV, US
82 NR, SW
83 CYRX
84 UE, KO
85 QR, TU
86 +×!£
87 =£O!
88 !@£=
89 =@O£
90 NUT
91 COME
92 DUNE
93 NOTE
94 12
95 8
96 9
97 13
98 21
99 7
100 13

Paper 6

1 autumn, weather
2 form, run
3 plate, glass
4 disperse, vanish
5 perimeter, edge
6 desert, abandon

7 swell, bulge
8 means, resources
9 allow, permit
10 underline, emphasise
11 LID
12 OUR
13 AND
14 OAK
15 ROW
16 weak
17 found
18 diminish
19 separate
20 increase
21 ra
22 se
23 th
24 el
25 st
26 te
27 grapefruit
28 download
29 bathe
30 asset
31 earring
32 BUTTER
33 DUST
34 PIN
35 WOOD
36 SUN
37 bet, link
38 sale, pitch
39 due, done
40 lip, lime
41 core, mats
42 spoil
43 fairly
44 country
45 wonder
46 pass
47 take, home, tomorrow
48 decorated, holly, Christmas
49 story, in, next
50 pay, tickets, see
51 tastes, sweet, sugar
52 outside
53 collar
54 time
55 wheel
56 shell
57 place
58 offensive, pleasant
59 maintain, neglect
60 endanger, protect
61 deteriorate, improve
62 swift, slow
63 NOTICE
64 FRIEND
65 CANDLE
66 MEALS
67 SHARING
68 PULP

69 BEAT
70 CLAY
71 HELM
72 PELT
73 ENACT

74–75

D	O	C	I	L	E
I		O		E	
S	A	N	D	E	D
U		F		W	
S	E	E	S	A	W
E		R		Y	

76–77

N	E	S	T	L	E
A		C		O	
T	I	R	A	D	E
U		O		G	
R	E	L	I	E	D
E		L		R	

78 MJXC
79 LEAN
80 EQJML
81 ROOF
82 JD
83 JY
84 XP
85 EP
86 SW
87 11:15 a.m.
88 10:45 a.m.
89 11:50 a.m.
90 12:05 p.m.
91 15
92 14
93 34
94 200
95 29
96 −O$@
97 ?O−@?
98 $?+=@
99 CLUB
100 BIAS

Paper 7

1 answer, reaction
2 example, model
3 rare, unusual
4 access, entrance
5 forecast, predict
6 ease
7 wrap
8 bout
9 kite
10 lean
11 some
12 conduct
13 outcome

Bond Verbal Reasoning Assessment Papers 11+-12+ years Book 2

14 dabbed
15 trustworthy
16 SON
17 WAR
18 MEN
19 TIN
20 LOG
21 k
22 e
23 g
24 t
25 r
26 complaint
27 mad
28 wet
29 decline
30 quick
31 waited, airport, flight
32 baby, November, Christmas
33 remember, capital, start
34 me, time, arrive
35 envelope, money, secretary
36 MALE, MILE
37 HARE, HALE
38 MOTH, MOTE
39 STEP, STEM
40 WIND, WINK
41 WART, WARS
42 FILL, FALL
43 it, the
44 like, can
45 Saturday, he
46 your, you
47 today, it's
48 clap
49 insert
50 spring
51 shock
52 cure
53 red
54 form
55 the
56 not
57 tea
58 hutch, stable
59 glue, commence
60 taste, sight
61 dip, track
62 throw, order
63 genuine, stopping
64 aeroplane
65 collect
66 carrot
67 complicated
68 restrict
69 bank, lair
70 bead, tear
71 slash, spoil
72 pay, track
73 cause, plod

74–75

P	L	E	A	T	S
L	■	N	■	E	■
A	D	D	I	N	G
N	■	O	■	O	■
T	O	W	E	R	S
S	■	S	■	S	■

76–77

E	N	E	R	G	Y
X	■	R	■	Y	■
C	A	M	E	R	A
I	■	I	■	A	■
S	A	N	I	T	Y
E	■	E	■	E	■

78 E
79 3
80 D
81 No
82 B
83 36
84 18
85 49
86 21
87 61
88 240
89 Megan can work when she is not in school.
90 I am unable to buy a card in that shop.
91 A cat has legs.
92 The boy plays sport.
93 I write stories with an ink pen.
94 ?×OO
95 !$?O
96 ?×O!+
97 CHEESE
98 SHARE
99 CHIEF
100 CASE

Paper 8

1 snow, frost
2 hero, timid
3 water, sieve
4 consist, constant
5 globe, footstep
6 famous, noted
7 puff, blow
8 jealousy, envy
9 count, matter
10 teach, guide
11 object
12 fire

13 whisper
14 price
15 break
16 RIM
17 RAY
18 HIT
19 RIP
20 PAN
21 oppose, favour
22 feeble, strong
23 entire, partial
24 invade, evacuate
25 failure, success
26 at
27 ne
28 er
29 am
30 ic
31 ly
32 sk
33 pleasure
34 forcefully
35 conform
36 stirring
37 inspire
38 suits, colour
39 with, an
40 on, collect
41 this, a
42 had, quite
43 queen
44 later
45 true
46 low
47 liquid
48 bold
49 glum
50 worn
51 main
52 gasp
53 rein
54 tile
55 treat
56 sore
57 vanish
58 leaves, yellow, Autumn
59 up, will, appointment
60 already, chosen, present
61 bring, in, night
62 feet, sofa, mud
63 AIR
64 POST
65 EAR
66 ARM
67 OVER
68 tan
69 ale
70 mash
71 frown
72 rise

73–74

	F		C		M
A	L	K	A	N	E
	U		R		D
D	R	A	P	E	D
	R		E		L
M	Y	R	T	L	E

75–76

H	O	L	L	O	W
O		A		U	
A	D	M	I	T	S
R		E		C	
D	I	N	E	R	S
S		T		Y	

77 SAND
78 DISH
79 MOUSE
80 SEAL
81 TRAM
82 A piano is a musical instrument.
83 Food is eaten at breakfast.
84 Summer is one of four seasons.
85 Water falls from the sky.
86 Rosie
87 Poppy
88 Gertie
89 Charlie
90 biscuits
91 GO, MI
92 HI, SR
93 GT, HS
94 TI
95 BY, FU
96 HKNO
97 FKPPGT
98 UJQGU
99 VCDNG
100 RCRGT

Paper 9

1 business, company
2 ignore, disregard
3 piano, guitar
4 clear, distinct
5 chair, stool
6 leave, rise
7 small, hard
8 just, devoted
9 rich, strange
10 bird, queen
11 y
12 r
13 l
14 n
15 k
16 w
17 RIG
18 ACT
19 ROB
20 TAG
21 PIN
22 everyone
23 nowhere
24 warrant
25 legend
26 contract
27 reasonable
28 SHELF
29 DIET
30 WOLF
31 REAL
32 DEAL
33 bell
34 rope
35 read
36 drip
37 tack
38 returns, about, eat
39 pupils, absent, illness
40 boat, harbour, sea
41 hot, give, drink
42 think, right, job
43 grasshopper, net
44 trepidation, concern
45 include, allow
46 words, address
47 wanting, respectful
48 head, first
49 bet, again
50 cub, learn
51 lash, feast
52 tint, paint
53 words, dictionary
54 that, both
55 go, remember
56 the, that
57 not, if
58 progress, advance
59 graze, scrape
60 separate, detach
61 bank, deposit
62 chief, main
63 BOLT
64 TIER
65 SYRUP
66 TOSS
67 BAGGY
68 SEAT

69–70

	P		A		C
Q	U	I	V	E	R
	D		E		U
A	D	O	R	N	S
	L		S		T
C	E	L	E	R	Y

71–72

S	H	O	U	L	D
A		Y		A	
I	N	S	A	N	E
N		T		D	
T	H	E	M	E	S
S		R		D	

73 D
74 E
75 1
76 E
77 MC
78 RL
79 QD
80 UB
81 43
82 10
83 70
84 31
85 33
86 Roses grow in soil.
87 Biscuits are eaten.
88 Computers are designed by people.
89 Some animals are small.
90 Wine is made from fruit.
91 SODWH
92 FKLOG
93 ERRN
94 GHVN
95 20
96 21
97 12
98 18
99 22
100 20

Paper 10

1 LEAP
2 FARES
3 CHEAT
4 SCREW
5 SWAP
6 grumble, moan
7 narrate, tell
8 subject, matter
9 crop, harvest
10 assorted, various
11 jewel, ring
12 leg, back
13 court, prison
14 planet, star
15 stop, discontinue
16 appeal
17 crush
18 vault
19 development

20 last
21 CAR
22 WIN
23 EAT
24 LAY
25 FIN
26 l
27 t
28 d
29 r
30 p
31 k
32 OVER
33 UP
34 AFTER
35 WIND
36 SOME
37 UNDER
38 because, computer, broken
39 write, forget, something
40 optician, remind, glasses
41 go, restaurant, pizza
42 December, skate, shop
43 sent
44 fit
45 set
46 team
47 bear
48 mother
49 month
50 absent
51 single
52 fruit
53 COLD

54 RING
55 TANK
56 STEAM
57 FLOW
58 TAKE
59 sped, feed
60 other, mend
61 her, leant
62 log, town
63 cane, bout
64 OT, RW
65 QJ, SH
66 ER, JI
67 NJ, MK
68 BY, EV
69 YZ, FG
70 DS, IN

71–72

S	T	R	I	K	E
P	■	E	■	E	■
R	I	S	I	N	G
A	■	U	■	N	■
Y	E	L	L	E	D
S	■	T	■	L	■

73–74

V	A	L	L	E	Y
O	■	I	■	L	■
L	E	T	T	E	R
U	■	T	■	V	■
M	E	L	T	E	D
E	■	E	■	N	■

75 David
76 £8
77 £7
78 £9
79 £5
80 –$@£
81 O$@£–
82 @£$O
83 TREAT
84 RULE
85 NEAR
86 LACE
87 There are some pictures in the book.
88 I could not speak to my friend.
89 Sometimes it's raining when my dog goes out.
90 I prefer other colours to red.
91 12
92 2
93 18
94 27
95 49
96 CZQSV
97 qhfp
98 RPTQ
99 jtl
100 WZB

Paper 6

Underline the two words which are the odd ones out in the following groups of words.

| **Example** | black | <u>king</u> | purple | green | <u>house</u> |

1	bounce	spring	autumn	leap	weather
2	sponsor	form	back	run	finance
3	fork	plate	glass	spoon	knife
4	disperse	appear	show	vanish	emerge
5	area	perimeter	edge	district	region

Underline the pair of words most similar in meaning.

| **Example** | come, go | <u>roam, wander</u> | fear, fare |

6	desert, abandon	fierce, fiend	pay, take
7	raw, cooked	realise, reassure	swell, bulge
8	doubtful, acceptable	means, resources	meek, arrogant
9	agree, upset	brief, long	allow, permit
10	admire, despise	underline, emphasise	calm, confused

Find the three-letter word which can be added to the letters in capitals to make a new word. The new word will complete the sentence sensibly.

Example The cat sprang onto the MO. <u>USE</u>

11 Kate loves to play on the SES at the playground. _____

12 My mum's started a computer CSE to brush up her office skills. _____

13 She always keeps her purse in her HBAG. _____

14 Nina was caught in the rain and got SED. _____

15 TH the ball to me! _____

Underline one word in the brackets which is most opposite in meaning to the word in capitals.

Example WIDE (broad vague long <u>narrow</u> motorway)

16 STRONG (powerful healthy weak athletic determined)

17 LOST (find found finding finds founded)

18 HEIGHTEN (increase improve ceiling prefer diminish)

19 UNITE (team combine marriage separate agreement)

20 CUT (chop hair increase shorten share)

(31)

Find two letters which will end the first word and start the second word.

Example	rea	(c h)	air

21 ext   (__ __)   bbit

22 mou   (__ __)   nse

23 dep   (__ __)   irty

24 kenn   (__ __)   astic

25 cru   (__ __)   uff

26 compe   (__ __)   rrible

6

Underline two words, one from each group, that go together to form a new word. The word in the first group always comes first.

Example   (hand, green, for)   (light, house, sure)

27 (peel, tall, grape)   (tree, skin, fruit)

28 (down, fast, loose)   (under, load, ten)

29 (bat, ball, show)   (wide, he, win)

30 (fur, draw, as)   (set, chart, nice)

31 (foot, neck, ear)   (pierce, pain, ring)

5

Find a word that can be put in front of each of the following words to make new, compound words.

Example	CAST	FALL	WARD	POUR	DOWN

32 FLY	CUP	FINGERS	MILK	_____
33 BIN	MAN	PAN	CART	_____
34 HEAD	STRIPE	POINT	PRICK	_____
35 LAND	LOUSE	WORK	PILE	_____
36 SHINE	RISE	STROKE	LIGHT	_____

5

Move one letter from the first word and add it to the second word to make two new words.

Example	hunt	sip	hut	snip

37 belt	ink	_____	_____
38 scale	pith	_____	_____
39 dune	doe	_____	_____
40 limp	lie	_____	_____
41 score	mat	_____	_____

5

Underline the one word in the brackets which will go equally well with both the pairs of words outside the brackets.

Example rush, attack   cost, fee   (price, hasten, strike, <u>charge</u>, money)

42 ruin, damage   overprotect, pamper   (ignore, indulge, baby, spoil, destroy)

43 quite, rather   honestly, legally   (really, fully, fairly, justly, properly)

44 farmland, rural   nation, state   (kingdom, people, landscape, outdoors, country)

45 puzzle, think   marvel, miracle   (question, excellent, wonder, wonderful, speculate)

46 give, hand   succeed, qualify   (transfer, allow, past, pass, graduate)

5

Complete the following sentences by selecting the most sensible word from each group of words given in the brackets. Underline the words selected.

Example The (<u>children</u>, books, foxes) carried the (houses, <u>books</u>, steps) home from the (greengrocer, <u>library</u>, factory).

47 We can (take, teach, tell) your friend (house, room, home) early (tomorrow, yesterday, breakfast).

48 I've (drawn, decorated, written) the house with (shells, daisies, holly) ready for (Easter, Halloween, Christmas).

49 My (word, number, story) has to be handed (on, in, off) (next, soon, following) week.

50 I'll (pay, sell, buy) you for the (tickets, children, friends) when I (ignore, hear, see) you.

51 Coffee (tastes, sounds, touches) too (hot, dark, sweet) if you add lots of (milk, powder, sugar).

5

Complete the following expressions by filling in the missing word.

Example Pen is to ink as brush is to <u>paint</u>.

52 Interior is to inside as exterior is to ＿＿＿＿＿.

53 Wrist is to cuff as neck is to ＿＿＿＿＿.

54 Thermometer is to temperature as clock is to ＿＿＿＿＿.

55 Petals are to flower as spokes are to ＿＿＿＿＿.

56 Orange is to peel as egg is to ＿＿＿＿＿.

57 Who is to person as where is to ＿＿＿＿＿.

6

Underline the two words, one from each group, which are the most opposite in meaning.

Example (dawn, <u>early</u>, wake)   (<u>late</u>, stop, sunrise)

58 (official, offensive, often)   (generally, pleasant, plead)

59 (sprint, abandon, maintain)   (run, certain, neglect)

60 (endanger, guard, assure)   (enclose, protect, promise)

61 (deteriorate, condition, declaration)   (deviate, reject, improve)

62 (speed, swift, street)   (slow, rapid, lane)

○ 5

B 16

Rearrange the muddled letters in capitals to make a proper word. The answer will complete the sentence sensibly.

    Example   A BEZAR is an animal with stripes.   ZEBRA

63 Please read the important IOCNTE below.   ————

64 I have known my best NRIFED since playgroup.   ————

65 Can I blow out the LADCNE now?   ————

66 Schools should provide healthy ELMAS for pupils.   ————

67 I don't mind RHISNAG with you.   ————

○ 5

B 18

Look at the first group of three words. The word in the middle has been made from the other two words. Complete the second group of three words in the same way, making a new word in the middle.

Example	PAIN	INTO	TOOK	ALSO	SOON	ONLY
68 DALE	LIME	MICE		COPE	————	LUMP
69 MUSE	TERM	DIRT		TYRE	————	DRAB
70 GIFT	GRIT	GIRL		EASY	————	CALL
71 TOPIC	COLT	WORLD		MUNCH	————	MEALS
72 PLUM	MELT	TIRE		CLIP	————	TALE
73 RAISE	SLIDE	DEALS		START	————	CLONE

○ 6

Fill in the crosswords so that all the given words are included. You have been given one letter as a clue in each crossword.

B 19

74–75

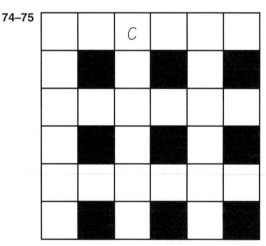

sanded, confer, docile, seesaw, disuse, leeway

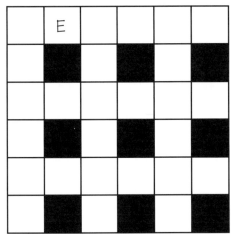

relied, tirade, nature, scroll,
nestle, lodger

4

A B C D E F G H I J K L M N O P Q R S T U V W X Y Z

78 If the code for NOTICE is JMRAXC, what is the code for ONCE? _____

79 If the code for ANGLE is PBVKH, what does KHPB stand for? _____

80 If the code for MILK is NHMJ, what is the code for DRINK? _____

81 If the code for DAY is WZB, what does ILLU stand for? _____

4

Fill in the missing letters. The alphabet has been written out to help you.

A B C D E F G H I J K L M N O P Q R S T U V W X Y Z

Example AB is to CD as PQ is to RS

82 XQ is to WP as KE is to ____

83 FH is to DJ as LW is to ____

84 BA is to WV as CU is to ____

85 IG is to KI as CN is to ____

86 FB is to UY as HD is to ____

5

My watch is 10 minutes slow. In 15 minutes it will say 11:20 a.m.

87 What is the correct time now? _____

88 What time did my watch say 20 minutes ago? _____

89 What will the correct time be 35 minutes from now? _____

90 What time will my watch say one hour from now? _____

4

Give the missing numbers in the following sequences.

Example	2	4	6	8	<u>10</u>	12

91	4	3	9	8	16	___	25
92	11	16	12	15	13	___	
93	56	49	43	38	___	31	
94	500	250	400	___	300	150	
95	15	17	21	23	27	___	

5

If the code for UNSOCIABLE is × ! $ £ = + O − ? @, what are the codes for the following words?

96 BASE _____   **97** LABEL _____   **98** SLICE _____

What do these codes stand for?

99 =?×− _____   **100** −+O$ _____

5

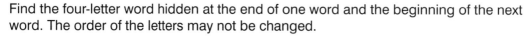

Now go to the Progress Chart to record your score!   Total   100

Paper 7

Underline the two words, one from each group, which are closest in meaning.

Example   (race, shop, <u>start</u>)   (finish, <u>begin</u>, end)

1 (answer, dramatic, drastic)   (ignore, reaction, normal)

2 (exact, enable, example)   (valuable, toy, model)

3 (rare, rather, stale)   (unusual, common, fresh)

4 (access, accident, excuse)   (exit, entrance, planned)

5 (prevent, forecast, rear)   (weather, predict, forefront)

5

Find the four-letter word hidden at the end of one word and the beginning of the next word. The order of the letters may not be changed.

Example   The children had bats and balls.   <u>sand</u>

6 Our dog catches fleas each time it sneaks next door.   _____

7 I notice how rapidly he answers the questions.   _____

8 Take the rhubarb out of the saucepan before it burns.   _____

9 Tick items off the list as you place them in our trolley.   _____

10 See the decorations sparkle and shimmer.   _____

5

Underline the two words, one from each group, that go together to form a new word. The word in the first group always comes first.

Example   (hand, <u>green</u>, for) (light, <u>house</u>, sure)

11 (so, add, can)   (verse, her, me)

12 (tap, con, snap)   (duct, fir, pea)

13 (past, high, out)   (word, up, come)

14 (beat, lay, dab)   (ten, bell, bed)

15 (set, sit, trust)   (tea, worthy, on)

Find the three-letter word which can be added to the letters in capitals to make a new word. The new word will complete the sentence sensibly.

Example   The cat sprang onto the MO.   USE

16 The PRIER escaped some time after lunch.   _____

17 She was UNAE of the trouble she had caused.   _____

18 Tourists often choose to visit the MONUT.   _____

19 She was CUTG the fabric carefully to make a dress.   _____

20 I've ordered some clothes from the new CATAUE.   _____

Find the letter which will complete both pairs of words, ending the first word and starting the second. The same letter must be used for both pairs of words.

Example   mea (<u>t</u>) able   fi (<u>t</u>) ub

21 dus (__) een   bac (__) ind

22 pal (__) cho   lac (__) agle

23 son (__) ate   rin (__) arage

24 coas (__) hick   bea (__) opic

25 towe (__) efer   wide (__) eal

Underline the one word in the brackets which will go equally well with both pairs of words or phrases outside the brackets.

Example   rush, attack   cost, fee   (price, hasten, strike, <u>charge</u>, money)

26 ailment, disorder   criticism, moan   (charge, disease, grumble, groan, complaint)

27 angry, fuming   devoted, keen   (furious, sensible, mad, enthusiastic, irrational)

28 damp, soaked   weak, soppy   (soft, dry, strong, wet, humid)

29 refuse, reject	dwindle, flag	(decrease, decay, degenerate, decline, deteriorate)
30 fast, brisk	clever, sharp	(quick, sluggish, ready, sudden, intelligent)

Complete the following sentences by selecting the most sensible word from each group of words given in the brackets. Underline the words selected.

> **Example** The (<u>children</u>, books, foxes) carried the (houses, <u>books</u>, steps) home from the (greengrocer, <u>library</u>, factory).

31 We (waited, wrote, sang) at the (concert, competition, airport) because our (ink, flight, effort) was delayed.

32 The (cot, baby, milk) was born in (November, morning, Saturday), a few weeks before (breakfast, bedtime, Christmas).

33 (Remember, Forget, Sorry) to put (bright, small, capital) letters at the (start, middle, end) of each sentence.

34 Let (you, me, those) know what (speed, rate, time) you'll (gone, arrive, came).

35 Hand the (envelope, stamp, pen) containing the ticket (winning, money, concert) to the school (playground, rules, secretary).

Change the first word into the last word by changing one letter at a time and making two new, different words in the middle.

> **Example** TEAK   <u>TEAT</u>   <u>TENT</u>   RENT

36 SALE	_____	_____	MILD
37 HARD	_____	_____	HOLE
38 BOTH	_____	_____	MITE
39 STOP	_____	_____	SEEM
40 WILD	_____	_____	LINK
41 WANT	_____	_____	BARS
42 FILE	_____	_____	FAIL

Find and underline the two words which need to change places for each sentence to make sense.

> **Example** She went to <u>letter</u> the <u>write</u>.

43 The dog scratched it door when the wanted to come in.

44 We like meet you earlier if you can.

45 Saturday grazed his knee playing rugby last he.

46 Did your like you present?

47 Today too cold it's to open the window.

Add one letter to the word in capital letters to make a new word. The meaning of the new word is given in the clue.

Example   PLAN   simple   <u>plain</u>

48 CAP   applaud   _____

49 INSET   put in   _____

50 SPRIG   bound   _____

51 SOCK   horrify   _____

52 CUE   remedy   _____

Change the first word of the third pair in the same way as the other pairs to give a new word.

Example   bind, hind   bare, hare   but, <u>hut</u>

53 raise, ear   night, tin   defer, _____

54 dive, dove   live, love   firm, _____

55 style, let   taper, era   heath, _____

56 swore, row   grate, tar   stone, _____

57 scarf, car   stare, tar   steam, _____

Complete the following sentences in the best way by choosing one word from each set of brackets.

Example   Tall is to (tree, <u>short</u>, colour) as narrow is to (thin, white, <u>wide</u>).

58 Rabbit is to (carrot, fur, hutch) as horse is to (hoof, stable, gallop).

59 Stick is to (tree, throw, glue) as start is to (end, commence, leave).

60 Tongue is to (taste, mouth, teeth) as eye is to (glasses, sight, colour).

61 Plunge is to (soar, raid, dip) as monitor is to (computer, disc, track).

62 Bowl is to (cereal, plate, throw) as command is to (boss, ruler, order).

63 Fake is to (money, pretend, genuine) as continuing is to (context, stopping, unchanging).

Underline the word in the brackets which goes best with the words given outside the brackets.

Example   word, paragraph, sentence   (pen, cap, <u>letter</u>, top, stop)

64 car, train   (brakes, engine, aeroplane, luggage, road)

65 assemble, gather   (scatter, manufacture, pupils, disperse, collect)

66 parsnip, onion   (vegetable, plum, grow, carrot, cook)

67 difficult, hard   (easy, advantage, contrast, complicated, separate)

68 limit, confine   (extend, vast, restrict, unending, free)

39

Move one letter from the first word and add it to the second word to make two new words.

Example	hunt	sip	hut	snip

69 blank   air   _____   _____

70 bread   tea   _____   _____

71 splash   soil   _____   _____

72 pray   tack   _____   _____

73 clause   pod   _____   _____

Fill in the crosswords so that all the given words are included. You have been given one letter as a clue in each crossword.

74–75

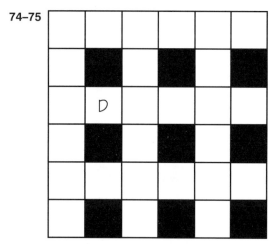

plants, endows, adding, tenors,
towers, pleats

76–77

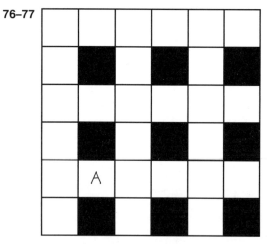

sanity, gyrate, excise, camera,
ermine, energy

A, B, C, D and E are cars parked in a straight line. A is not first in the line, but it is in front of at least three cars. B is directly behind C. C is two cars behind D. D is not last in the line.

B 25

78 Which car is last in the line? _____

79 How many cars are in front of B? _____

80 Which car is first in the line? _____

81 Are there any cars behind E? _____

5

82 If D and C swap places, which car is now behind D? _____

B 23

Give the missing numbers in the following sequences.

Example	2	4	6	8	_10_	12
83 27	—	46	57	69	82
84 9	20	11	—	13	16
85 25	81	36	64	49	—
86 48	84	42	24	12	—
87 93	82	73	66	—	58
88 2	10	40	120	—	240

6

Read the first two statements and then underline one of the four options below that must be true.

B 25

89 'Megan goes to school. She has a part-time job.'

Megan does her job every day.

Megan only works at weekends.

Megan can work when she is not in school.

Megan wants to work full time.

Read the first two statements and then underline one of the four options below that must be true.

90 'I need to buy a birthday card. The shop is closed.'

I'm going to a birthday party.

I will have to buy the card tomorrow.

I am unable to buy a card in that shop.

I will make a card myself.

Read the first two statements and then underline one of the four options below that must be true.

91 'A cat is an animal. Animals have legs.'

A cat has fur.

A cat has four legs.

A cat has legs.

A cat has kittens.

Read the first two statements and then underline one of the four options below that must be true.

92 'A boy plays football. Football is a sport.'

The boy likes football.

The boy plays for his school team.

The boy plays sport.

The boy wears football boots.

Read the first two statements and then underline one of the four options below that must be true.

93 'I write stories. I use an ink pen.'

I sometimes make mistakes.

I like using an ink pen.

Everyone in our class uses an ink pen.

I write stories with an ink pen.

○ 5

If the code for FRANCHISE is ? × $ £ / + @ ! O, what are the codes for the following words?

B 24

94 FREE _____   **95** SAFE _____   **96** FRESH _____

What do these codes stand for?

97 / + O O ! O _____   **98** ! + $ × O _____

99 / + @ O ? _____   **100** / $! O _____

○ 7

Now go to the Progress Chart to record your score!   Total ○ 100

Paper 8

Underline the two words which are the odd ones out in the following groups of words.

B 4

Example	black	king	purple	green	house
1 sledge	snow	frost	aeroplane	boat
2 bold	hero	fearless	timid	courageous
3 bottle	water	vase	kettle	sieve
4 consist	consent	constant	permit	allow
5 globe	circuit	course	track	footstep

○ 5

(42)

Underline the two words, one from each group, which are closest in meaning.

B 3

Example (race, shop, <u>start</u>) (finish, <u>begin</u>, end)

6 (famous, unknown, common) (wrote, noted, exciting)

7 (pull, puff, spent) (push, blow, saved)

8 (jagged, sad, jealousy) (smooth, envy, jolly)

9 (count, maths, opposed) (subtract, support, matter)

10 (pupil, teach, study) (confuse, lessons, guide)

5

Underline the one word in the brackets which will go equally well with both the pairs of words outside the brackets.

B 5

Example rush, attack cost, fee (price, hasten, strike, <u>charge</u>, money)

11 thing, article argue, protest (oppose, motive, objective, object, item)

12 blaze, heat shoot, explode (electrify, inspire, dismiss, sparkle, fire)

13 murmur, sigh hint, gossip (breathe, divulge, whisper, whistle, suggestion)

14 cost, amount consequences, sacrifice (charge, expense, penalty, outlay, price)

15 pause, stop destroy, ruin (rest, shatter, break, demolish, crack)

5

Find the three-letter word which can be added to the letters in capitals to make a new word. The new word will complete the sentence sensibly.

B 22

Example The cat sprang onto the MO. <u>USE</u>

16 Most children attend a PARY school close to their home. _____

17 She SPED air freshener in the kitchen after frying the onions. _____

18 The ARCECT has drawn the plans for our extension. _____

19 His football shirt has distinctive black and white STES. _____

20 Her father recently started a new job with a different COMY. _____

5

Underline the pair of words most opposite in meaning.

B 9

Example cup, mug coffee, milk <u>hot, cold</u>

21 opposite, different oppose, favour spray, surge

22 feeble, strong brilliant, excellent cram, stuff

23 contest, struggle	entire, partial	expended, spent
24 illustrate, represent	plot, conspiracy	invade, evacuate
25 faded, dim	people, folk	failure, success

Find two letters which will end the first word and start the second word.

Example   rea (c h) air

26 form   (—— ——)   tract

27 pru   (—— ——)   glect

28 upp   (—— ——)   upt

29 stre   (—— ——)   ount

30 garl   (—— ——)   icle

31 light   (—— ——)   ing

32 bri   (—— ——)   ate

Underline two words, one from each group, that go together to form a new word. The word in the first group always comes first.

Example   (hand, green, for)   (light, house, sure)

33 (plea, sea, left)   (sent, sure, hand)

34 (force, inn, great)   (full, fully, stall)

35 (par, on, con)   (ant, form, down)

36 (set, pick, stir)   (all, ring, tea)

37 (in, tall, stay)   (too, spire, bell)

Find and underline the two words which need to change places for each sentence to make sense.

Example   She went to <u>letter</u> the <u>write</u>.

38 That suits really colour you.

39 I've made with appointment an the optician.

40 We can on my parents collect the way.

41 I sent her this text a morning.

42 She didn't do had as well as she quite expected.

Complete the following expressions by filling in the missing word.

B 15

Example Pen is to ink as brush is to <u>paint</u>.

43 Man is to woman as king is to _____.

44 Before is to earlier as after is to _____.

45 Sweet is to sour as false is to _____.

46 Up is to down as high is to _____.

47 Wood is to solid as water is to _____.

5

Find the four-letter word hidden at the end of one word and the beginning of the next word. The order of the letters may not be changed.

B 21

Example The children had bats and balls. <u>sand</u>

48 I've taken the drab old curtains down. _____

49 The gravy was going lumpy in the saucepan. _____

50 Do you notice how ornate the decorations are? _____

51 They do drama in the hall. _____

52 She had been neglecting aspects of her work since it became harder. _____

5

Remove one letter from the word in capital letters to leave a new word. The meaning of the new word is given in the clue.

B 12

Example AUNT an insect <u>ant</u>

53 RESIN strap to control a horse _____

54 TITLE covers roof, floor or walls _____

55 THREAT attend to _____

56 SCORE painful _____

57 VARNISH die out _____

5

Complete the following sentences by selecting the most sensible word from each group of words given in the brackets. Underline the words selected.

B 14

Example The (<u>children</u>, books, foxes) carried the (houses, <u>books</u>, steps) home from the (greengrocer, <u>library</u>, factory).

58 The (leaves, stones, plates) turn (blue, sparkly, yellow) every (Autumn, birthday, minute).

59 Hurry (up, down, across)! We (were, will, are) be late for our (choice, place, appointment).

60 He has (already, soon, presently) (chosen, walked, eaten) your (present, mile, hunger).

61 We (deliver, bring, introduce) our cat (in, on, below) every (dozen, season, night).

62 Take your (feet, scarf, pen) off the (sofa, hook, shoes) – you'll get (drink, mud, hair) on it.

Find a word that can be put in front of each of the following words to make new, compound words.

Example	CAST	FALL	WARD	POUR	<u>DOWN</u>
63 TIGHT	STRIP	LINE	LOCK		_____
64 SCRIPT	CARD	CODE	MARK		_____
65 PLUG	SHOT	RING	PIECE		_____
66 PIT	REST	LOCK	CHAIR		_____
67 CAME	CROWD	LAP	SEAS		_____

Change the first word of the third pair in the same way as the other pairs to give a new word.

Example bind, hind   bare, hare   but, <u>hut</u>

68 stern, ten   force, ore   stain, _____

69 weak, awe   real, are   lean, _____

70 rapid, raid   cheat, chat   marsh, _____

71 rough, tough   test, vest   drown, _____

72 mad, dame   elf, flee   sir, _____

Fill in the crosswords so that all the given words are included. You have been given one letter as a clue in each crossword.

73–74

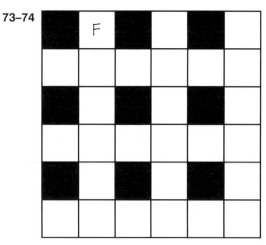

myrtle, meddle, draped, carpet, alkane, flurry

46

hoards, lament, admits, hollow, outcry, diners

Look at the first group of three words. The word in the middle has been made from the other two words. Complete the second group of three words in the same way, making a new word in the middle of the group.

	Example	PAIN	INTO	TOOK	ALSO	SOON	ONLY
77	CAROL	CARE	PEDAL		SONAR	_____	IDEAL
78	SOIL	LIFE	FEUD		GRID	_____	SHUT
79	SPITE	TRIPS	PRESS		DRUMS	_____	SOLVE
80	LUCK	CLAP	PART		EASY	_____	LATE
81	SIDED	SAID	IDEAS		TAMED	_____	ALARM

Read the first two statements and then underline one of the five options below that must be true.

82 'The girl likes music. Her favourite musical instrument is the piano.'

       The girl plays the piano well.

       The girl likes listening to music.

       Keys on a piano are black and white.

       A piano is a musical instrument.

       The girl can read music.

Read the first two statements and then underline one of the five options below that must be true.

83 'Breakfast is a meal. A meal is an occasion when food is eaten.'

       Most people eat cereals or toast for breakfast.

       Breakfast is eaten in the morning.

       Food is eaten at breakfast.

       Orange juice is a popular drink.

       Breakfast is followed by lunch.

Read the first two statements and then underline one of the five options below that must be true.

84 'Summer is a season. There are four seasons.'

It is hot in summer.

Autumn comes after summer.

Christmas is in the winter.

Summer is one of four seasons.

People go on holiday in the summer.

Read the first two statements and then underline one of the five options below that must be true.

85 'Rain is made of water. Rain falls from the sky.'

Rain makes puddles.

Water comes from rivers.

Snow falls from the sky.

Heavy rain causes floods.

Water falls from the sky.

Poppy and Gertie are dogs. Charlie and Rosie are cats. Gertie and Rosie like tinned food. Charlie and Poppy prefer biscuits. Gertie and Charlie have short hair; Poppy and Rosie have long hair. Only Gertie likes eating bones.

86 Which cat has long hair? _____

87 Which dog doesn't like bones? _____

88 Which dog prefers tinned food? _____

89 Which cat is short-haired and eats biscuits? _____

90 What sort of food does Poppy like? _____

Give the missing pairs of letters in the following sequences. The alphabet has been written out to help you.

A B C D E F G H I J K L M N O P Q R S T U V W X Y Z

Example	CQ	DQ	EP	FP	_GO_	_HO_
91 CS	EQ	___	IM	KK	___	
92 BC	YX	EF	VU	___	___	
93 DW	EV	FU	___	___	IR	
94 AT	PE	CR	RG	EP	___	
95 AZ	___	CX	DW	EV	___	

4

B 25

5

B 23

5

(48)

If the code for DOG is FQI, what are the codes for the following words? The alphabet has been written out to help you.

A B C D E F G H I J K L M N O P Q R S T U V W X Y Z

96 FILM _____   **97** DINNER _____   **98** SHOES _____

99 TABLE _____   **100** PAPER _____ ?

Now go to the Progress Chart to record your score! **Total** ◯ 100

Paper 9

Underline the two words in each line which are most similar in type or meaning.

	Example	dear	pleasant	poor	extravagant	expensive
1	aid	city	business	cottage	company
2	alarm	ignore	greet	advise	disregard
3	hockey	piano	match	listen	guitar
4	clear	usual	rinse	distinct	vague
5	chair	table	wardrobe	crate	stool

Complete the following sentences in the best way by choosing one word from each set of brackets.

Example   Tall is to (tree, short, colour) as narrow is to (thin, white, wide).

6 Come is to (appear, leave, due) as fall is to (hurt, asleep, rise).

7 Massive is to (small, elephant, size) as soft is to (pretty, hard, easy).

8 Fair is to (hair, school, just) as faithful is to (believers, devoted, disloyal).

9 Broke is to (ruined, faulty, rich) as familiar is to (family, strange, people).

10 Nest is to (twigs, den, bird) as palace is to (country, queen, luxury).

Find the letter which will complete both pairs of words, ending the first word and starting the second. The same letter must be used for both pairs of words.

Example   mea (t) able   fi (t) ub

11 fanc (__) oung   tr (__) ard

12 rea (__) ate   hei (__) ock

13 fai (__) ead   curtai (__) ow

14 brai (__) asty   crow (__) ature

15 brin (__) ill   cas (__) ick

16 bre (__) ant   gro (__) hole

49

Find the three-letter word which can be added to the letters in capitals to make a new word. The new word will complete the sentence sensibly.

B 22

Example The cat sprang onto the MO. USE

17 The new curtains really BHTEN up the room. _____

18 The FORY has closed, so lots of people will have to look for new jobs. _____

19 Put all the clothes back in the WARDE. _____

20 The garden beside the old COTE was very overgrown. _____

21 The DRIPG tap kept me awake last night. _____

5

Underline two words, one from each group, that go together to form a new word. The word in the first group always comes first.

B 8

Example (hand, green, for) (light, house, sure)

22 (every, ever, never) (were, less, one)

23 (no, now, some) (won, all, here)

24 (awe, drop, war) (rain, rant, full)

25 (cape, leg, skill) (all, end, able)

26 (in, race, con) (end, tract, salt)

27 (tab, reason, rise) (sing, able, up)

6

Rearrange the letters in capitals to make a new word. The new word has something to do with the first words.

B 16

Example spot soil SAINT STAIN

28 ledge for support flat piece of wood FLESH _____

29 lose weight food TIDE _____

30 wild dog hunts in a pack FLOW _____

31 genuine existing EARL _____

32 negotiate hand out LEAD _____

5

Find the four-letter word hidden at the end of one word and the beginning of the next word. The order of the letters may not be changed.

B 22

Example The children had bats and balls. sand

33 The label lets the consumer read product information. _____

34 Never open our door to strangers. _____

35 This area definitely improved when the houses were built. _____

36 They stored ripe apples in the cellar. _____

37 His curt acknowledgement of the problem didn't help. _____

5

Complete the following sentences by selecting the most sensible word from each group of words given in the brackets. Underline the words selected.

Example　　The (<u>children</u>, books, foxes) carried the (houses, <u>books</u>, steps) home from the (greengrocer, <u>library</u>, factory).

38 He usually (returns, sees, follows) from work (through, concerning, about) 6 p.m., in time to (put, repair, eat).

39 Three (dogs, drivers, pupils) were (strict, absent, bored) from my class due to (danger, blame, illness).

40 The (train, boat, car) left the (platform, garage, harbour) and headed out to (air, rail, sea).

41 As it's (hot, weak, dim) today, I'll (hit, cross, give) you money for extra (fuel, drink, paper).

42 I don't (frighten, deliver, think) that I have the (right, left, straight) skills for the (job, meal, way).

5

Underline the two words which are the odd ones out in the following groups of words.

Example　　black　　<u>king</u>　　purple　　green　　<u>house</u>

43	tennis	cricket	grasshopper	football	net
44	wonder	surprise	trepidation	amazement	concern
45	include	exclude	allow	bar	eliminate
46	catalogue	words	dictionary	address	atlas
47	responsive	wanting	willing	respectful	forthcoming

5

Move one letter from the first word and add it to the second word to make two new words.

Example　　hunt　　sip　　*hut*　　*snip*

48	heard	fist	_____	_____
49	beat	gain	_____	_____
50	club	earn	_____	_____
51	leash	fast	_____	_____
52	taint	pint	_____	_____

5

Find and underline the two words which need to change places for each sentence to make sense.

Example　　She went to <u>letter</u> the <u>write</u>.

53 She needed her words to find the dictionary.

54 That the cat and dog sleep in both bed.

55 Go to switch the light off before you remember to bed.

56 Put the back in that box.

57 I'll leave a message not you're if there.

5

Underline the two words, one from each group, which are closest in meaning.

B 3

Example (race, shop, <u>start</u>) (finish, <u>begin</u>, end)

58 (progress, work, cover) (attack, advance, change)

59 (eat, graze, playful) (scrape, trouble, naughty)

60 (own, separate, live) (combine, detach, fix)

61 (coins, money, bank) (spend, debt, deposit)

62 (senior, plain, chief) (junior, firm, main)

5

Look at the first group of three words. The word in the middle has been made from the other two words. Complete the second group of three words in the same way, making a new word in the middle.

B 18

Example PA<u>IN</u> INTO <u>TOO</u>K ALSO <u>SOON</u> ONLY

63 DATE DIAL LILT BLUE _____ VOTE

64 KITE STIR SPUR VEIN _____ TOUR

65 LITRE TRAIL TRAWL PUSHY _____ TYRES

66 BEAN BINS SUIT TIPS _____ SPOT

67 RINSE SENSE UPSET RUGBY _____ BEGAN

68 POKE KEEP BEAK TILE _____ HATS

6

Fill in the crosswords so that all the given words are included. You have been given one letter as a clue in each crossword.

B 19

69–70

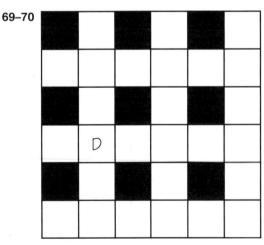

adorns, crusty, puddle, quiver, averse, celery

landed, insane, should, oyster,
themes, saints

A, B, C, D and E are five towns. C is due west of B and due north of A. A is east of E and B is due south of D.

73 Which town is north east of C? _____

74 Which town is furthest west? _____

75 How many towns are north of B? _____

76 Which town is south west of C? _____

Fill in the missing letters. The alphabet has been written out to help you.

A B C D E F G H I J K L M N O P Q R S T U V W X Y Z

Example   AB is to CD as PQ is to R̲S̲

77 JS is to IR as ND is to ___

78 KC is to HF as UI is to ___

79 QF is to SH as OB is to ___

80 BM is to GJ as PE is to ___

Underline the wrong number on each line.

Example	3	6	<u>10</u>	12	15
81 16	24	32	43	48	56
82 10	20	31	42	53	64
83 96	84	70	60	48	36
84 66	54	44	36	31	26
85 42	20	35	33	28	30

Read the first two statements and then underline one of the five options below that must be true.

86 'A rose is a plant. Plants grow in soil.'

       Roses are red.

       Roses grow in the garden.

       Rose bushes have thorns.

       Roses grow in soil.

       Rose stems can be put in a vase.

Read the first two statements and then underline one of the five options below that must be true.

87 'Biscuits are food. Food is eaten.'

       People enjoy biscuits with a cup of tea.

       Some biscuits are covered with chocolate.

       Biscuits are eaten.

       Biscuits are stored in a tin.

       Food can be just a snack.

Read the first two statements and then underline one of the five options below that must be true.

88 'A computer is a machine. People design machines.'

       You can play games on a computer.

       Computers are used in schools.

       A computer has a keyboard.

       Some people don't have a computer.

       Computers are designed by people.

Read the first two statements and then underline one of the five options below that must be true.

89 'Kittens are animals. Kittens are small.'

       Kittens drink milk.

       Some kittens scratch.

       Some animals are small.

       Kittens like to play.

       Kittens grow into cats.

Read the first two statements and then underline one of the five options below that must be true.

90 'A grape is a fruit. Wine is made from grapes.'

> Fruit is the opposite of vegetable.
> Grapes grow on bushes.
> People drink wine.
> Other fruits can be used to make wine.
> Wine is made from fruit.

5

B 24

If the code for FRAGILE is IUDJLOH, what are the codes for the following words? The alphabet has been written out to help you.

A B C D E F G H I J K L M N O P Q R S T U V W X Y Z

91 PLATE _____   **92** CHILD _____

93 BOOK _____   **94** DESK _____

4

B 26

If A = 2, B = 3, C = 4, D = 5, E = 6 and F = 7, find the sum of the following words by adding the letters together.

95 FADE _____   **96** CEDE _____   **97** EBB _____

98 FED _____   **99** BEEF _____   **100** DEAF _____

6

Now go to the Progress Chart to record your score!   **Total** 100

Paper 10

Rearrange the letters in capitals to make another word. The new word has something to do with the first two words.

B 16

Example	spot	soil	SAINT	STAIN
1 jump		soar	PEAL	_____
2 travel cost		charges	SAFER	_____
3 fraud		deceive	TEACH	_____
4 twist		fasten	CREWS	_____
5 exchange		trade	PAWS	_____

5

Underline the two words, one from each group, which are closest in meaning.

B 3

Example (race, shop, start)   (finish, begin, end)

6 (grumble, customer, try)   (praise, illness, moan)

7 (reading, play, narrate)   (stage, role, tell)

8 (subject, school, future)   (matter, history, present)

9 (sow, crop, vegetable)   (harvest, sell, increase)

10 (similar, assorted, chocolate)   (various, plain, sophisticated)

Underline the two words which are the odd ones out in the following groups of words.

Example	black	king	purple	green	house

11 gold	jewel	silver	ring	copper
12 elbow	leg	wrist	back	shoulder
13 assess	court	judge	prison	consider
14 Saturn	Mercury	planet	Mars	star
15 stop	discontinue	proceed	continue	persist

Underline the one word in the brackets which will go equally well with both the pairs of words outside the brackets.

Example   rush, attack   cost, fee   (price, hasten, strike, <u>charge</u>, money)

16 request, plea   fascinate, tempt   (prayer, charm, interest, appeal, attract)

17 smash, break   overpower, overcome   (crunch, crush, crusade, grind, cause)

18 jump, leap   cellar, tomb   (bound, spring, cavern, chamber, vault)

19 growth, advance   event, situation   (result, outcome, development, expansion, improvement)

20 closing, final   continue, remain   (stay, fade, latest, extreme, last)

Find the three-letter word which can be added to the letters in capitals to make a new word. The new word will complete the sentence sensibly.

Example   The cat sprang onto the MO.   <u>USE</u>

21 They entertained each other with SY stories, but were too frightened to switch off the light!   _____

22 She ran straight to the SGS when they arrived at the park.   _____

23 He wore his red SWSHIRT to the football match.   _____

24 My train was DEED, so I missed the meeting.   _____

25 I DEITELY want to see the movie.   _____

Find the letter which will complete both pairs of words, ending the first word and starting the second. The same letter must be used for both pairs of words.

B 10

     Example   mea (t) able   fi (t) ub

26 basi (__) ight   rai (__) eak

27 cas (__) ide   boo (__) ale

28 gree (__) ial   len (__) ust

29 poo (__) ice   bea (__) oad

30 cha (__) late   soa (__) lain

31 par (__) eep   pic (__) ilt

 6

Find a word that can be put in front of each of the following words to make new, compound words.

B 11

     Example   CAST   FALL   WARD   POUR   DOWN

32 LEAF   ACT   TIME   WEIGHT   _____

33 FRONT   HILL   HOLD   KEEP   _____

34 WARDS   TASTE   NOON   THOUGHT   _____

35 SURFING   PIPE   SWEPT   SCREEN   _____

36 HOW   TIMES   ONE   BODY   _____

37 COOK   COVER   GO   LINE   _____

 6

Complete the following sentences by selecting the most sensible word from each group of words given in the brackets. Underline the words selected.

B 14

     Example   The (<u>children</u>, books, foxes) carried the (houses, <u>books</u>, steps) home from the (greengrocer, <u>library</u>, factory).

38 I couldn't do my homework (under, because, into) the (kettle, TV, computer) was (fast, new, broken).

39 (Write, remember, study) the list down so you don't (think, avoid, forget) (nothing, something, sometime).

40 The (dentist, office, optician) telephoned to (say, explain, remind) me to collect my (cups, glasses, drinks).

41 Can we (go, leave, depart) to the (cinema, pool, restaurant) for a (chip, pizza, popcorn)?

42 Every (July, March, December), there is an ice rink in our town centre and children (eat, ride, skate) while their parents (shop, dig, swim) for Christmas.

 5

Change the first word of the third pair in the same way as the other pairs to give a new word.

Example   bind, hind   bare, hare   but, _hut_

43 black, back   smack, sack   spent, _____

44 fast, sat   fact, cat   lift, _____

45 board, rob   wound, now   tease, _____

46 loaf, foal   read, dear   meat, _____

47 man, mean   met, meet   bar, _____

5

Complete the following expressions by filling in the missing word.

Example   Pen is to ink as brush is to _paint_.

48 Brother is to sister as father is to _____.

49 Hour is to minute as year is to _____.

50 Bitter is to sweet as present is to _____.

51 Two is to double as one is to _____.

52 Daisy is to flower as peach is to _____.

5

Look at the first group of three words. The word in the middle has been made from the other two words. Complete the second group of three words in the same way, making a new word in the middle.

Example   PAIN   INTO   TOOK   ALSO   _SOON_   ONLY

53 PEACE   BASE   BRUSH   PROUD   _____   CALLS

54 FABLE   MALT   EMPTY   LIONS   _____   BRAGS

55 CARTON   TRAP   HAMPER   SNATCH   _____   TINKLE

56 FRUIT   THIRD   HANDS   GAMES   _____   THEME

57 COTTON   TORE   FOREST   COFFEE   _____   SLOWER

58 KEEN   KITE   LIST   TEAR   _____   BACK

6

Move one letter from the first word and add it to the second word to make two new words.

Example   hunt   sip   _hut_   _snip_

59 speed   fed   _____   _____

60 mother   end   _____   _____

61 hear   lent   _____   _____

62 long   tow   _____   _____

63 canoe   but   _____   _____

5

Give the two missing pairs of letters in the following sequences. The alphabet has been written out to help you.

A B C D E F G H I J K L M N O P Q R S T U V W X Y Z

Example	CQ	DQ	EP	FP	*GO*	*HO*
64 CH	FK	IN	LQ	___	___	
65 KP	MN	OL	___	___	UF	
66 AV	NE	CT	LG	___	___	
67 RF	QG	PH	OI	___	___	
68 AZ	___	CX	DW	___	FU	
69 GH	JK	NO	ST	___	___	
70 TC	UB	WZ	ZW	___	___	

7

Fill in the crosswords so that all the given words are included. You have been given one letter as a clue in each crossword.

71–72

rising, yelled, strike, sprays, result, kennel

73–74

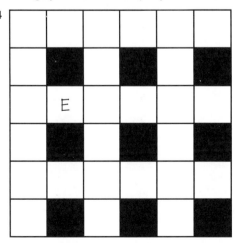

melted, little, eleven, valley, letter, volume

4

Mark, Chiman, David and Simon all earn weekly pocket money. Mark earns the least, £6 less than Simon. David earns twice as much as Chiman, who earns £1 more than Mark. Simon earns £13 per week.

75 Who earns the most? _____

76 How much does Chiman earn? _____

77 How much does Mark earn? _____

78 How much less than David does Mark earn? _____

79 If David gives Chiman half of his money, how much less than Simon does David now earn? _____

5

If the code for CONGRATULATE is ? + ! × − $ @ * O $ @ £, what are the codes for the following words?

80 RATE _____   **81** LATER _____   **82** TEAL _____

What do these codes stand for?

83 @ − £ $ @ _____   **84** − * O £ _____

85 ! £ $ − _____   **86** O $? £ _____

7

Read the first two statements and then underline one of the four options below that must be true.

87 'There are pages in the book. There are pictures in the book.'

      Each page has a picture.

      There is no writing in the book.

      The book is for children.

      There are some pictures in the book.

Read the first statement and then underline one of the four options below that must be true.

88 'I left a message for my friend.'

      My friend was out.

      My friend was busy.

      I could not speak to my friend.

      I sent a text to my friend.

Read the first two statements and then underline one of the four options below that must be true.

89 'I walk my dog every day. My dog doesn't like rain.'

    My dog won't go out when it rains.

    I take an umbrella when it rains.

    Sometimes it's raining when my dog goes out.

    I take my dog out when it's stopped raining.

Read the first two statements and then underline one of the four options below that must be true.

90 'Red isn't my favourite colour. Today I am wearing a red sweater.'

    I don't like my sweater.

    Someone else gave me the sweater.

    I hardly ever wear the sweater.

    I prefer other colours to red.

4

If A = 2, B = 3, C = 4, D = 5 and E = 6, give the answers to these calculations.

B 26

91 $B \times C =$ _____

92 $(E + A) \div C =$ _____

93 $(D^2 + B^2) - C^2 =$ _____

94 $B \times (C + D) =$ _____

95 $(2A + 3B) + E^2 =$ _____

5

A B C D E F G H I J K L M N O P Q R S T U V W X Y Z

96 If the code for REST is TCUR, what is the code for ABOUT? _____

B 24

97 If the code for CASTLE is ghfpqr, what is the code for LAST? _____

98 If the code for ENACT is DOZDS, what is the code for SOUP? _____

99 If the code for ADEPT is pctjl, what is the code for PET? _____

100 If the code for BED is YVW, what is the code for DAY? _____

5

Now go to the Progress Chart to record your score!   Total   100

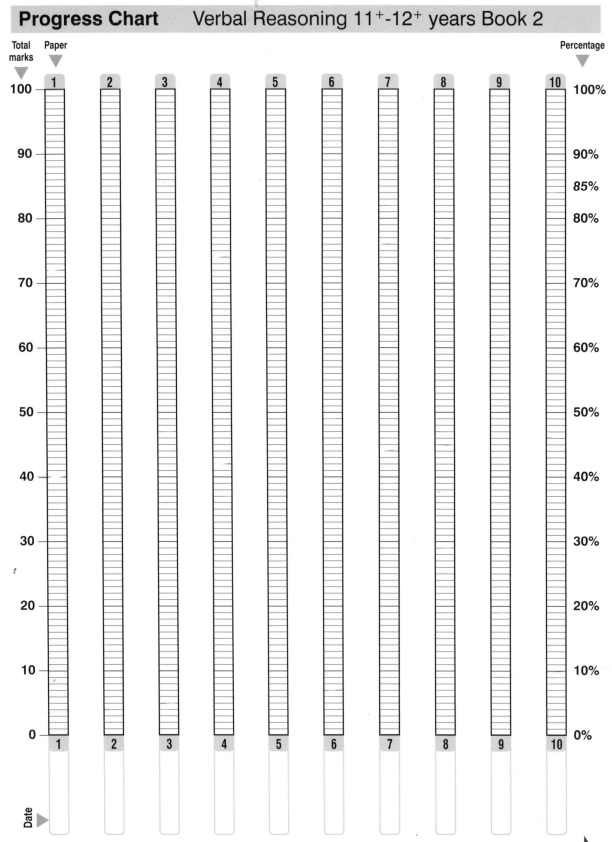

Progress Chart   Verbal Reasoning 11⁺-12⁺ years Book 2

Total marks

Paper

Percentage

| 1 | 2 | 3 | 4 | 5 | 6 | 7 | 8 | 9 | 10 |

100

90

80

70

60

50

40

30

20

10

0

100%
90%
85%
80%
70%
60%
50%
40%
30%
20%
10%
0%

Date

When you've finished the book use the Next Step Planner